THE ART OF BROADSWORD FIGHTING FOR STAGE AND SCREEN

The Art of Broadsword Fighting for Stage and Screen provides historical and contemporary techniques and styles for the safe training and use of the European broadsword in a theatrical setting.

This book starts with a brief breakdown of the history of broadswords, the time periods associated with their use, and the influences of historical masters and their manuscripts. After the brief history section, this book presents the basic techniques of broadsword fighting, starting with grip and body postures. Readers will then move fluidly into the basic actions of cuts, parries, blocks, and disarms. During this process, actors explore the connection between body and weapon and start learning the elements of storytelling through choreography. Special attention is given throughout the text on techniques which need to be approached in a physically and/or mentally safe way by directors, choreographers, performers, teachers, and students. The final chapter focuses on choreographing a fight and utilizing all the material previously covered in this book, with special notes for actors, directors, and teachers about what makes a good fight, how to keep it safe, and how to create the "wow factor" in choreography.

The Art of Broadsword Fighting for Stage and Screen is intended for directors, choreographers, actors, students of acting, martial artists, and enthusiasts of stage combat and historical martial arts.

Erick Vaughn Wolfe is an international fight director with over 25 years' experience in film, TV, Theatre, Musical Theatre, Opera, and Ballet, working in stunts, fight choreography, intimacy, directing, and movement. He is a member of the Stage Directors and Choreographers Society (SDC) and is a certified teacher with both the British Academy of Dramatic Combat (BADC) and the Academy of Performance Combat

(APC). He earned his BFA in Performance from the University of Central Oklahoma and his MFA in Film and Theatre Directing from the University of New Orleans. After running his own stage combat training school for 10 years, Erick traveled around teaching combat and movement across the United States and the United Kingdom, before entering into teaching at the university level, where his focus is on leadership for the Arts in academia, theatre, and film studies.

THE ART OF BROADSWORD FIGHTING FOR STAGE AND SCREEN

An Actor's and Director's Guide to Staged Violence

Erick Vaughn Wolfe

NEW YORK AND LONDON

Designed cover image: Master1305/Shutterstock.com

First published 2024
by Routledge
605 Third Avenue, New York, NY 10158

and by Routledge
4 Park Square, Milton Park, Abingdon, Oxon, OX14 4RN

Routledge is an imprint of the Taylor & Francis Group, an informa business

© 2024 Erick Vaughn Wolfe

The right of Erick Vaughn Wolfe to be identified as author of this work has been asserted in accordance with sections 77 and 78 of the Copyright, Designs and Patents Act 1988.

All rights reserved. No part of this book may be reprinted or reproduced or utilised in any form or by any electronic, mechanical, or other means, now known or hereafter invented, including photocopying and recording, or in any information storage or retrieval system, without permission in writing from the publishers.

Trademark notice: Product or corporate names may be trademarks or registered trademarks, and are used only for identification and explanation without intent to infringe.

Library of Congress Cataloging-in-Publication Data
Names: Wolfe, Erick Vaughn, author.
Title: The art of broadsword fighting for stage and screen:
an actor's and director's guide to staged violence / Erick Vaughn Wolfe.
Description: New York, NY: Routledge, 2024. |
Includes index.
Identifiers: LCCN 2023047679 (print) | LCCN 2023047680 (ebook) |
ISBN 9781032356051 (hardback) | ISBN 9781032356044 (paperback) |
ISBN 9781003327622 (ebook)
Subjects: LCSH: Stage fencing.
Classification: LCC PN2071.F4 W65 2024 (print) |
LCC PN2071.F4 (ebook) | DDC 792.02/8—dc23/eng/20231214
LC record available at https://lccn.loc.gov/2023047679
LC ebook record available at https://lccn.loc.gov/2023047680

ISBN: 978-1-032-35605-1 (hbk)
ISBN: 978-1-032-35604-4 (pbk)
ISBN: 978-1-003-32762-2 (ebk)

DOI: 10.4324/9781003327622

Typeset in Joanna
by codeMantra

To all who have picked up a sword and been captured by its spirit.

"Let this my sword report what speech forbears"

— Henry VI, Part 2 *Act* 4, *Scene* 10
by *William Shakespeare*

CONTENTS

	Foreword by Christian Tobler	xi
	Acknowledgments	xiii
1	Introduction	1
2	Taking History to the Stage and Screen	4
3	Types of Swords	9
4	The Elements of Theatrical Violence	14
5	Wards and Guard Positions	19
6	Footwork and Body Dynamics	45
7	The Basic Cuts	63
8	Blocks and Parries	83
9	Active Blocks and Attacks on the Blade	98

10	Advanced Cuts and Actions	114
11	Killing Actions and Adding Flair	127
12	Final Thoughts for Actors and Directors	142

    Glossary   153
    Appendix A: Organizations   176
    Appendix B: Suppliers   178
    Appendix C: Additional Resources   180
    Index   183

FOREWORD

Christian Tobler

Moviegoers thrilling to the famous rapier duel in *The Princess Bride* may recall the two swordsmen bragging of their knowledge of fencing moves derived from various masters – Bonetti, Capo Ferro, Thibault, and Agrippa. What they wouldn't likely know is that these were actual masters of the sword of the 16th and 17th centuries. Their names belong to history, though the fencing displayed in the movie, for the most part, does not.

Watching a movie swordfight as an actual swordsmanship instructor is often frustrating, much in the way that the whirring and beeping of computers on the big screen infuriates anyone who has spent any time programming them. Having taught German medieval swordsmanship for many years – and done my share of professional software development – I can relate in both matters. I suppose the beeping is excused by the need to have something happening audibly beyond the clicking of keyboards; the lack of realism in swordfights is explained away by the need for safety, and, in some cases, a belief that a "real fight" would be either quickly over or boring.

The reality of combat, and its potential in dramatized violent, is quite different. Period combat involves a number of very exciting techniques, and choreographed fights produced by such groups as the Adorea Fight Team are chock full of documentable actions, thrilling, and safely performed. Now, of course, such videos are produced by very talented martial artists, and not every film can populate its characters with actors who possess that skillset.

This is where Erick Wolfe comes in.

In this volume, Erick has created a methodology for bridging the gap between historic combat, as documented in surviving medieval and Renaissance treatises, and the world of safely performed theatrical violence. With a foot in each of the realms of Historical European Martial Arts (HEMA) and stage combat, he draws from the works of the masters of the broadsword, whether that weapon is the German or Italian longsword or its later true two-handed offspring. He, thus, presents a form of stage combat I would characterize as "historically informed".

Covering guards and stances, basic cuts, and dramatic effect, his method strikes an important and difficult balance between proper body mechanics, realistic choreography, excitement, and, above all, safety. As Erick puts it, the goal is to "keep the actors safe, but put the characters in danger".

So, here's to a day when more realistic, historically inspired, but still exciting swordplay makes to the movie screen or stage. Erick Wolfe has done his part with this offering to ensure that this does indeed come to pass.

Christian Henry Tobler
Oxford, Connecticut – June 2023

ACKNOWLEDGMENTS

This book could not have been possible without all the wonderful teachers, educators, actors, directors, mentors, students, colleagues, and friends who lent me their insight, openness, knowledge, compassion, time, energy, resources, and critiques. There are far too many to name here, but thank each and every one of you.

Thanks to my team at Routledge, Lucia Accorsi and Stacy Walker. Without your support, pushing, and kindness, this book never would have been completed. You are both rockstars!

Thanks to my technical editor, Steaphen Fick. Without who's help, this book would not have become what it is today. Your insights, knowledge, and experience make me always strive to better myself and my art.

Thank you, Christian Tobler, who I have been fortunate to know for many years now. Your expertise and insights into the German Fight Manuscripts led the path for me and developing this book. It has been a great honor to know you and get the chance to work with you.

And finally, to my family and friends, thank you for your patience and support.

1

INTRODUCTION

The first stage weapon I ever worked with was the broadsword. It was the mid-1990s, and I had just joined a group of medieval reenactors who all performed at the local Medieval festival once a year. They would do swordfights and period accurate dances in period accurate costumes. Notice, I did not say period accurate fighting with period accurate swords. The fighters in this group were not professionally trained in stage combat, nor were they the kind of fighters you would see in armor bashing each other about. They were just enthusiast who loved swords, dancing, and reenactment. It was this group that sparked the fire that would have me traveling around the world learning from any instructor who would give me the time of day, working with the early pioneers and researchers of HEMA (Historical European Martial Arts), and eventually lead me to becoming an internationally certified teacher.

Although my training through the years took many forms and many different styles of weapons, I always came back to the broadsword. There is something beautiful, graceful, and deadly about the European broadsword. I mention European because many cultures around the world have a version of a broad sword. Japan has the **Katana**, China has the **Dao**, Egypt has the **Khepesh**, along with the Moroccan **Flyssa**, the Sudanese **Kasskara**, the Nigerian **Takouba**, and so on across the globe. Yet, I will limit this book to focusing on the European "Broadsword", more specifically the hand-and-a-half sword, or bastard sword. I will go into more detail about terminology in the chapter *Taking History to the Stage and Screen*. Also in that chapter, I will examine and look at the importance of historical manuscripts, those who wrote them, the historical terms (including the misapplication of the term "broadsword"), and different styles of fighting. Afterward, in the chapter *Types of Swords*, I will go over the types and styles of swords, and the difference in regions and time periods, along with movie references and modern sword masters. In the following chapter *The Elements of Theatrical Violence*, I give a lengthy discussion on safety, elements of theatrical fighting, and sword maintenance.

Once we get through the history and nomenclature of our art, we will dig into the techniques, starting with the chapter on *Wards and Guard Positions*. This is followed by the foundation of all fighting arts, *Footwork and Body Dynamics*. In these two chapters, we will begin our journey of blending historical elements into the standard theatrical combat styles that actors may be accustomed too. For the historical community, we will be adding safety and theatricality to moves you may already know from historical manuscripts. Either way, this is where we start the merging of elements which leads to building more dynamic and entertaining fights.

The chapters *Basic Cuts* and *Blocks and Parries* get us started with actions of the sword. Here, we focus more on the traditional side of theatrical combat to build the skills needed for advanced techniques to be performed with a partner safely. The following chapters, *Active blocks and Attacks on the Blade* and *Advanced cuts and Actions*, get into the deep end of applying historical sword fighting to the fight. Here, we will be adding all kinds of historical actions to our fighting style. Then, we close out the work on the broadsword with *Killing Actions and Adding Flair* from both historical and completely physically dynamic actions. This is where we get to play and keep the audience engaged with not only the fight but also the story we are telling with our actions.

Finally, to close out the book, in the chapter *Final Thoughts for Actors and Directors*, I will talk about tips, tricks, and general advice for actors and directors when it comes to staging and performing fights for film or theatre. Real-world advice for those who need to know it before they engage in this activity. This section will be followed by the Glossary and the Appendixes.

I hope you enjoy working your way through this book as much as I enjoyed creating it. It is a passion of mine to bring historical elements to all areas of the theatrical violence and stage combat weapon systems. And while I feel I did a decent job of laying the groundwork for historical European sword fighting to be integrated with stage combat, this book is designed as an introduction. Feel free to reach out to me at @baldmanfighting and let me know your thoughts, or what weapon system you would like to see in the future.

2

TAKING HISTORY TO THE STAGE AND SCREEN

One of the major reasons for wanting to draft this book is due to the limited amount of historical sword fighting I have seen on stage and screen. That is not to say there are not some beautiful historically inaccurate fights performed in the past, nor am I saying there are not some good historically accurate fights. And, I do understand that not all historical techniques, which were designed for killing, can be easily transferred to the stage and screen. However, what was driving me crazy was watching broadswords used as heavy bludgeoning tools or used like rapiers, when in fact the broadsword is a beautifully flowing weapon with actions all its' own, that when choreographed properly can tell a delightful story.

However, for us to tell this story, we must first go back and look at the methods, manuals, and masters of the time when these swords were taught and used for personal, judicial, and military use. Below I have curated a small list of what I feel are the best ten manuscripts and masters of the longsword style of combat from the 1400–1500s. The list is arranged in chronological order and is not to be considered a conclusive list of what is considered valuable or worthy. This abbreviated list of historical manuscripts is more about the ones that I find most influential in recreating historical methods for modern theatrical combat.

My Top 10 European Historical Manuscripts and Masters

Before I start this list, I would like to talk about **Johannes Liechtenauer**. Liechtenauer was a **fencing master** (here, fencing is referring to the use of all weapons and martial arts of the period) from Germany. There does not seem to be much about his life or works that still exist, but what we do have is a long poem of rhyming couplets, which have been ascribed to him by later authors, called the **Zettel** (recital). Now, I am not going to go too deep into this, as many other great authors have done the work on translating and researching Liechtenauer's work (especially the great work done by Christian Tobler, you know, they guy who wrote the forward to this book). However, I do want to say that Liechtenauer was a major influence on many fencing masters of the time and later, and many of them reference his work inside their own manuscripts. Along with the masters below, we will also be examining some of his techniques later in this book.

Starting off the list is the Italian manual from the early 1400s by **Fiore de'i Liberi**, titled *Fior di Battaglia* (The Flower of Battle, and known as Flos Duellatorum). The original manuscript (MS Ludwig XV 13) is in the J. Paul Getty Museum in Los Angeles, California. This brilliantly illustrated manuscript covers wrestling, dagger, single-hand sword, two-handed sword, sword and axe fighting in armor, and even mounted fighting. There are four versions of this manuscript known currently, and each has a nick name, the one above is known as the Getty (J. Paul Getty Museum), there is also the Pisani-Dossi (Museo archeologico Villa Pisani Dossi in Corbetta, Italy), Morgan (Pierpont Morgan Library in New York), and Florius "de Arte Luctandi" (Bibliothèque Nationale de France).

Following in the tradition of Fior de'i Liberi is the Italian fencing master **Philippo di Vadi Pisano** (1425–1501). Vadi's manuscript from the 1480s titled *De Arte Gladiatoria Dimicandi* (On the Art of Swordsmanship) is beautifully illustrated showing the use of sword, pole weapons, spear, dagger, and armored combat.

Next is the beautifully collected work by an unknown author from about the mid-1400s. The **Codex Wallerstein** is a collection of illustrations and text covering dagger, wrestling, long sword, short sword, and even longshield dueling. It is believed the book was compiled by **Paulus Hector Mair** in 1556 (more on him later).

Another anonymous work from about the same time in Germany is the MS KK5013 in the Kunsthistorisches Museum in Vienna, Austria. This work, along with several others with similar art and style, is commonly referred to as the **Gladiatoria** group. This German manuscript is a wonderfully color-illustrated manual covering spear, sword, dagger, and wrestling all in armor. Another manuscript, MS Germ.Quart.16, at the Biblioteka Jagiellońska in Kraków, Poland, has many of the same style images as the German manuscript but also adds in longshields, sword and shield, messer and shield, and staffs.

At about this same time in the mid-1400s, **Hans Talhoffer** was producing another set of major works. Talhoffer has at least six illustrated **Fechtbücher,** or "Fight Books" attributed to him, with his most popular ones dating from 1443, 1459, and 1467. His manuscripts cover all sorts of fighting, including armored fighting, long sword, dagger, wrestling, staffs, pole weapons, mounted fighting, sword and buckler, flail, longshield, messer, and judicial duels. He also has a section in a couple of his books between a man (in a waist deep pit with a club) and wife (standing on the ground swinging a 5lb stone in a veil).

Jörg Wilhalm was a German fencing master who produced several manuscripts and treaties in the late 1400s and early 1500s. Many of these illustrations follow the same style as we have seen in Talhoffer, and it is believed Wilhalm may have collected and reprinted existing works and just set his name in them as an owner's mark. His work includes fighting with swords, dussack, staff, dagger, and sword and buckler.

The first person I want to bring to light in the 1500s is **Paulus Hector Mair**. Mair was born in 1517 in Augsburg, Germany, which is also where he was hung to death as a thief 62 years later on December 10, 1579. However, during his life, he had spent a great amount of time (and money) collecting fencing treaties and manuscripts. Through his collecting and work, he was able to publish several manuscripts, most of which were reproductions of previous treaties, with beautiful illustrations and notes. His books covered all kinds of fighting from scythe, flail, staff, mixed weapons, grappling, rapier, poleaxe, long sword, armored fighting, mounted fighting, and much more.

From Germany we go down to Italy, with a fantastically illustrated manuscript on sword play by **Achille Marozzo** (1484–1553), entitled **Opera Nova** (New Work), which was published in 1536. In many of the illustrations for this work we see either a single fighter or a pair of combatants demonstrating everything from guard positions to attacks and counters. Weapons covered in this work include knife, pole weapons, long sword, sword and dagger, sword and shield, along with sword and buckler/cape.

Another influential manual was the German fencing treaty known as the **Goliath Fechtbuch**, created around 1540. This manuscript contains some exquisitely decorated illustrations covering several styles of combat collected from various masters who all seem to be in the tradition of Johannes Liechtenauer. This book derives its name from the inside cover illustration of the encounter between David and Goliath from biblical lore. This manuscript covers long sword, daggers, grappling, and mounted fighting.

In continuing to look at some beautifully illustrated treaties, look no further than the works of **Joachim Meyer** (1537–1571). Not to be one lacking words, his last work is titled: **Gründtliche Beschreibung, der freyen Ritterlichen unnd Adelichen kunst des Fechtens, in allerley gebreuchlichen Wehren, mit vil schönen und nützlichen Figuren gezieret und fürgestellet** ("A Thorough Description of the Free, Chivalric, and Noble Art of Fencing, Showing Various Customary Defenses, Affected and Put Forth with Many Handsome and Useful Drawings"). The illustrations in this book are breathtaking, showing fighters engaged in many styles of sword play with vivid colors and use of perspective styles with fighters both in the foreground and background. Some illustrations have spectators looking on from the background, or people having a meal. This book covers sword, dussack, rapier, dagger, wrestling, staff, and pole weapons.

Closing Comments

The above list is just a small example of the hundreds of known historical text dealing with sword combat. I wanted to provide a selection I felt could be easily accessible to the beginning artist, as many books and reproductions have been made and published over the works described above, which you can find in the back of this book under *Appendix C: Additional Resources*. Thankfully, every year more researchers and artists are finding new texts or discovering different approaches to the manuscripts and sharing their work. So, for a 600-year-old art, it still is alive and swinging (again, pun intended).

3

TYPES OF SWORDS

In Shakespeare's play *Romeo and Juliet*, Lord and Lady Capulet have this exchange:

CAPULET
What noise is this? Give me my long sword, ho!
LADY CAPULET
A crutch, a crutch! why call you for a sword?

The Use of the Term "Broadsword"

The term broadsword has a very *broad* meaning (pun intended). In modern-day stage combat, we use the term to refer to the hand-and-a-half sword, sometimes referred to as a "bastard sword" as it was a cross between a single-hand sword and the two-handed sword, or longsword of late medieval/early renaissance European era.

However, we are using the term *broadsword* incorrectly.

Lord Headley says it best in his book, *Broadsword and Single-Stick* from 1890

> The word "Broad-sword" may be taken to include all kinds of cut-and-thrust swords. It is the generic term for ship's cutlass, infantry sword, and heavy cavalry sabre, which are all cutting weapons, and, though varying in length and curvature of blade, can be used for pointing.

So yes, we should just call them swords, single-hand sword, hand-and-a-half sword, or long-sword/two-handed sword. But colloquial language is evolving and constantly changing things around, we can just call them broadswords.

Ewart Oakeshott Typology

The historian and illustrator Ewart Oakeshott (1916–2002) established in his 1960 book **The Archaeology of Weapons: Arms and Armor from Prehistory to the Age of Chivalry**, what would later become known as "The Oakeshott Typology". This was a way to define and catalog the various swords of the 11th through 16th centuries in Europe based upon their physical characteristics. This newly created typology would allow the categorization of swords into 13 main types, labeled X through XXII. These 13 would be a continuation of Sir Mortimer Wheeler's work from his 1927 book **London and the Vikings.** Here, Wheeler refined the typology of Jan Petersen's 26 types and sub types of the Viking swords from his 1919 book **De Norske Vikingsverd** ("The Norwegian Viking Swords"), down to seven types, labeled I through XII. Oakeshott would also create two transitional types to merge these lists together, creating Types VIII and IX.

At this point, you may be asking "How does this typology affect us?", well to be honest, it doesn't. This is more of a tool for archeologists and historians than for martial artists and performers. However, this can be a good reference if you want to make sure the swords you are using in your production are historically accurate to the time and place of the show.

For general guidelines, we can use an oversimplification of breaking it down into two main regional timelines: European Medieval and European Renaissance, followed by generalizations down into Single-Hand, Hand-and-a-Half, and Two-Handed.

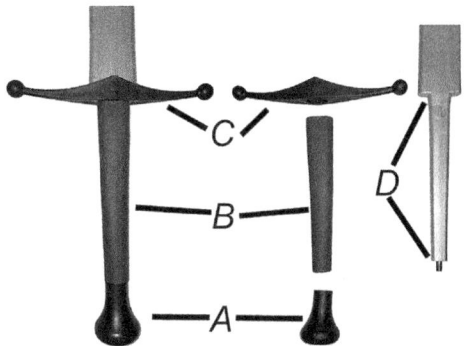

Figure 3.1 Parts of the Hilt

A Sword and Its' Parts

Hilt

Parts of the Hilt:

A. **Pommel**: A piece of metal located at the base of the grip which serves the dual purpose of locking the different parts of the weapon together and acting as a counterweight to the blade.
B. **Grip**: The part of the handle normally held by the hand
C. **Cross-guard**: The part of a sword's hilt, the bar that crosses the blade above the handle which protects the hands.
D. **Tang**: The base of a sword blade that the hilt, handle, and pommel attach to.

Blade

Parts of the Blade:

1. **Central Ridge**: The part of the swords blade. Swords with diamond cross-sections had a central ridge running along the middle of the blade just before the point, this helped strengthen the blade.
2. **Edge**: The Edge is the cutting surface of a blade that extends from point to shoulder/hilt.
3. **Point**: The intersection of the front (edge) and back of the blade intended for penetration or detailed cutting.

TYPES OF SWORDS

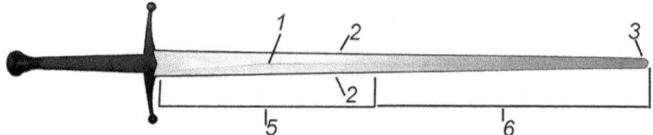

Figure 3.2 Blade Parts

4. **Fuller** (not shown): The grove in the sword blade used to help strengthen the blade.
5. **Forte** (Strong): The base or strongest part of a sword blade.
6. **Foible** (Weak): The tip or weakest part of a sword blade

Edge

On double-edged swords, there is a distinction between True Edge (Front Edge) and False Edge (Back Edge). This distinction is created when you are holding your sword in front of you. The true edge is your forward edge, in line with your front knuckles, and your false edge is the edge facing your body, in line with your forearm.

Modern Training Swords

The improvements in commercially available training swords have grown significantly since the expansion and popularity of Historical European Martial Arts (HEMA) training groups and competitions. Now, you can get training swords in foam, high-density polymers, wood, and blunt metal (steel and aluminum). You can find more of these resources in Appendix B – Suppliers.

Theatrical/Film Swords

There used to be very few commercial broadswords available for theatrical use. And of those, very few were even close to historically accurate. Now, there are many more companies and individuals who produce theatrical and film quality swords from bargain priced all the way to very expensive. You can find more of these resources in Appendix B – Suppliers.

Closing Comments

For historians and archaeologists, it is easy to get lost in the minute details of a weapon and its origin. For the actor and director, we can simplify the choices down quickly to what fits the period and location. There is a great amount of variety in the European swords produced during the Medieval and Renaissance periods. Thanks to the growth of HEMA organizations, researchers, scholars, and enthusiasts, finding training material and weapons of both quality and affordability has never been better than it is today. For more information on sword makers and where to buy equipment, check out Appendix B: Weapon Suppliers.

4

THE ELEMENTS OF THEATRICAL VIOLENCE

Safety: First and Foremost

It has been so many years now that I do not remember who I first heard it from, but one of my first lessons in safety was the simple phrase: "The more out of control the character is, the more in control the actor has to be". I have kept that in the forefront of all my work and pass it to every actor and student I work with.

If you read this book chapter by chapter, you will get a sense of repetition about one principle of stage combat that I feel is the most important aspect, safety. Safety is at the heart of everything we do when we teach, choreograph, or perform any type of violence for stage or screen. A safe choreography is also a repeatable choreography. We should never allow an actor to be in danger, physically or emotionally. We should never allow anyone, including the cast, crew, or audience to be in any form of danger. I take this to heart, and it has been my guiding principle my entire career. Acted aggression is a dangerous business on its own. Actors can get caught up in the moment, adrenaline can spike, or countless other things can go wrong. Add to these moments a weapon, especially a weapon like a sword, and the possibility for accidents or injuries double. Therefore, we must always keep safety first and foremost in all our work.

However, a fight must not look excessively safe to the audience. If the audience does not feel a sense of connection to the characters and is not engaged or invested into the dangers of the fight for the characters, then we are defeating our second rule: Serve the story. Notice I said characters and not actors. Keep the actors safe but put the characters in danger. A fight, or moment of choreography, must be a part of the total story being told. It must fit in seamlessly with the previous actions and flow into the next segment of the show. We must continue the audience's willing suspension of disbelief. Fights are used for many reasons in a story, such as setting conflicts (think opening fight of *Romeo & Juliet*) or sending a protagonist on their journey (*Star Wars A New Hope*), or the final resolution of building conflict, which includes too many to name here. Whatever the reason for the inclusion of the fight, it must fit within the world the writer and director have created. All too often I have witnessed a fight, usually choreographed by someone just starting out, that just sticks out from the rest of the show. It is either too slow, too far apart, the actors break character and are just mindlessly performing choreography with no acting behind it, or the choreographer wants to put in all the cool and flashy moves they can think of for that wow factor. First, good job on keeping everyone safe, you followed the first rule. However, there is no story or continuity to the action. Therefore, you failed the second rule. Yet, to be honest, this is the hardest part of fight direction to learn. When I was first starting out, I was guilty of all those actions at one time or another, but fortunately, I had people around who helped and mentored my growth as a choreographer and director. The technical elements, the actual stage combat, take work and practice under the guidance of a qualified teacher. Learning how to be a fight director or choreographer takes time and understanding. You need to fully understand story structure, lines of sight, vocalization, intent, collaboration with all the designers and directors, performers' physical and emotional boundaries, and never forget a little bit of stage magic. All of this goes into a choreography to tell a good story.

A final note on safety I would like to address before you get started has to do with the equipment you use. All combat weapons should have no cutting edge or sharp point. Many times, I have seen companies or choreographers use whatever is available, and all too often these weapons were never meant for stage combat purposes. There are companies and prop makers out there who do make theatrical weapons, and there are places you can rent quality equipment if you cannot afford to purchase what you need. A list of these companies can be found in Appendix B. There is also some great work being done by prop masters all over the world who are using wood, plastics, rubber, and aluminum to make believable, but safe, stage and screen weaponry.

In all the exercises contained in this book, we always use wood or polymer training swords, which can be acquired easily from many companies on the internet at very affordable prices. Once the choreography is learned and the actors are safely repeating the choreography, we trade out the practice weapons for the show weapons and start the process over at a slow pace, letting the performers get adjusted to the new props.

Partnering

If you are new to theatrical violence, the term "partnering" may be foreign to you.

Working with a partner is a necessity in choreography. How you work with the individual or individuals is called partnering. Being a good partner is very important. Fights have a dialogue between the combatants, and it is this physical conversation that must play out to the audience. The physical, emotional, and visual elements are vital for dynamic choreography. Working together you will manage the timing of the action, the intentions behind your character's actions and reactions, the emotions of gaining advantage and losing it, the points of focus, and the objectives of the moment.

Take care of yourself and your partner in the fight. Be aware constantly of how they are doing, and how you are doing. Communicate openly with each other during rehearsals and check in regularly. Be safe.

Distance

The understanding of distance in theatrical combat is extremely important. We can look at distance in two ways when working on choreography.

The first is the actors' distance, the space between two performers. The second is the character distance, the space between two characters. Now, these may sound like the same thing, but they are not. The actors can be out of distance from contacting their partner, but the characters can be in distance for an attack to happen, which will need a reaction from the other character. This stage distance is where many of our actions take place. We are selling the threat of danger to the audience but keeping the performers safe.

There are times when moves will be done in distance so that the performers can make contact for actions like cuts, grabs, disarms, and other actions. However, with proper staging or camera angles, you can make stage distance look like the performers are close enough for actions to land, and the threat believable. However, there will be times when you want your characters to be out of distance from each other for actions like probing and false attacks, or big sweeping gestures with the sword to keep the other character away from them.

Speed

I will talk a lot about speed and the speed of actions in this book. I always recommend learning an action slowly at first. Take your time, build your skill, and understand the action. Once you have mastered the technique and mastered the choreography, then you can bring it up to performance speed.

Performance speed is the pace at which the fight looks believable, the actions can be seen by the audience, and the actors have full control of their moves. Too fast, and the audience can't keep track of what is happening, and neither can your partner. Too slow, and the audience doesn't believe in the fight and is not buying the fact that the characters are in danger.

Tempo, the speed of the individual movements, must be always controlled by the performers. Some moves may be choreographed to be performed quickly, while others may be deliberately slow. This visible and audible variable creates the rhythm of the fight. If all the actions are rushed, or too slow, we lose this rhythm.

When working a fight, I always have performers "walk-through" the actions. Here, they are just learning the choreography and are putting the moves together in a slow controlled fashion. Once the performers have mastered the actions, reactions, sounds, and emotions of the scene, we will begin bringing it up to performance speed, by moving it to half-speed. Half-speed, also referred to as training speed, has the performers flowing through the action as they would in the performance, combining all the elements together and finding the rhythm of the fight. Once half-speed is under full control, we will bump the tempo up to ¾ speed. This is where the fight is just slightly slower than the performance speed. Here, we start seeing the dynamics of the choreography taking its full shape in the space. **Warning**: This is also where performers may try to speed up. So be careful to keep the pace. After this is smooth and controlled, we will bring the fight up to performance speed. Here, the moves should look natural and believable. Even a fight that is designed to look sloppy or messy is clearly seen and believed by the audience and the performers and keeps everyone safe.

Weapon Maintenance

A safe fight starts with safe equipment. As I stated earlier, no weapon should ever have a sharp edge or point. There is never an excuse to put a person in real physical danger. Proper equipment must be used and maintained. Every rehearsal and performance should start and end with a prop check. Metal weapons can develop nicks and burrs along the edge that will need to be filed down. Wooden props may splinter or crack and need to be carefully inspected to prevent injury or weapon breakage. Hard plastic weapons may also develop nicks or cracks along the blade, or even warp due to excessive use or storage.

Another issue with theatrical swords is rust. Blades must be inspected and cleaned before and after every use.

Always have at least one spare prop sword in case one gets damaged during a show run. **Never use a damaged prop on stage.**

This book does not replace qualified instruction from a recognized organization's certified teacher.

5

WARDS AND GUARD POSITIONS

Figure 5.1 Opening Image of Actor with Sword on Guard

DOI: 10.4324/9781003327622-5

Holding the Sword

As with any weapon or tool a proper grip is crucial. When working with swords, or any prop weapon, we want to make sure the performer has a solid grasp of the prop. Many beginning students tend to hold the weapon very tightly, as in a "death grip". This grip is indicated by grabbing the handle in the same way you would a hammer with excessive energy applied to holding the weapons, where the hand and forearm are extremely tense. This excess energy will hamper your use of the weapon on stage and cause your arms to tire out and be less controlled, and may even cause injury. In all the grips described below, you should maintain a controlled but relaxed grip, firm but soft. A grip that is both secure enough not to let the sword go flying out of their hands, but also not so tight that their hands and forearms are stressed and cramping. Sword fighting is very fluid, and a relaxed grip will help you achieve this fluidity needed to create dynamic and exciting fights.

A note to left-handed performers, all directions are for right-hand dominant performers, left-hand dominant performers should adjust as needed to mirror the actions illustrated.

Single-Hand Grip

Figure 5.2a illustrates the overhand single-hand grip, with the thumb and fingers wrapped around the top of the handle, but underneath the cross guard.

Figure 5.2b illustrates the underhand single-hand grip, with the thumb and fingers wrapped around the handle, but the thumb is toward the pommel and the pinky closer to the cross guard.

Hand-and-a-Half Grip

Figure 5.2c illustrates the hand-and-a-half grip, with the right hand's thumb and fingers wrapped around the top of the handle, and the left hand placed underneath the right, with the lower fingers overlapping the pommel.

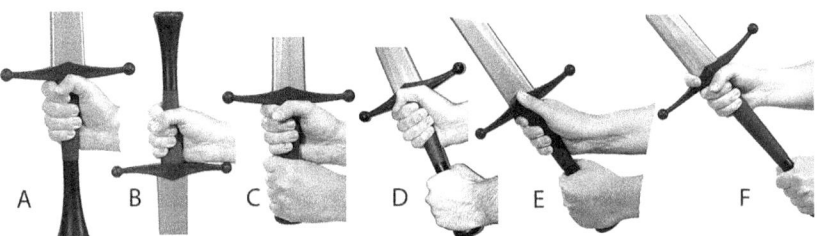

Figure 5.2 Grips

Two-Handed Grip

Figure 5.2d illustrates the two-handed grip, with the right hand's thumb and fingers wrapped around the top of the handle, but underneath the cross guard, and the left hand holding close to the bottom of the handle close to the pommel, allowing space between the two hands.

Thumbing-the-Blade

Figure 5.2e illustrates the two-handed grip while "thumbing-the-blade", with the right hand's thumb extended to the flat of the blade and fingers wrapped around the top of the handle, but underneath the cross guard, and the left hand holding close to the bottom of the handle close to the pommel, allowing space between the two hands.

Wrapping a Finger Over the Guard

Figure 5.2f illustrates the two-handed grip, with the right hand's index finger wrapped around the top of the cross guard, and the left hand holding close to the bottom of the handle close to the pommel, allowing space between the two hands.

This position is not recommended on swords without finger rings due to the increased possibility of injury to the finger owing to a blade sliding down and crushing or cutting the wrapped finger.

Final Note on Hands

When describing certain actions or hand placements, the terms **Pronated** and **Supinated** are used.

Pronated – Hand position where the palm is facing down.
Supinated – Hand position where the palm is facing up.

A Note on General Body Posture

As a performer, understanding your body is essential. Although each guard position is different, you should remember these key factors:

- Your knees should always have a slight bend.
- Never lock your knees when standing in a guard stance, even extended legs will have a bend.
- Keep your shoulders relaxed, this provides an ease of movement and prevents fatigue.
- Remember to keep a firm but relaxed grip on your sword.
- Keep a slight bend in your elbows, even if the guard or block has your arms at full extension.

Figure 5.3 illustrates the lines of attack and defense, used here to exemplify the areas of the body.

The four zones of attack and defense:

High Inside (Figure 5.3a)
High Outside (Figure 5.3b)
Low Inside (Figure 5.3c)
Low Outside (Figure 5.3d)

The Base Stance

Start standing, with your feet shoulder width apart, step forward in a straight line with your left foot until the heel of your left foot is in line with the toes of your right foot (reversible depending on the guard or the performer). Your hips and shoulders should be focused forward.

WARDS AND GUARD POSITIONS   23

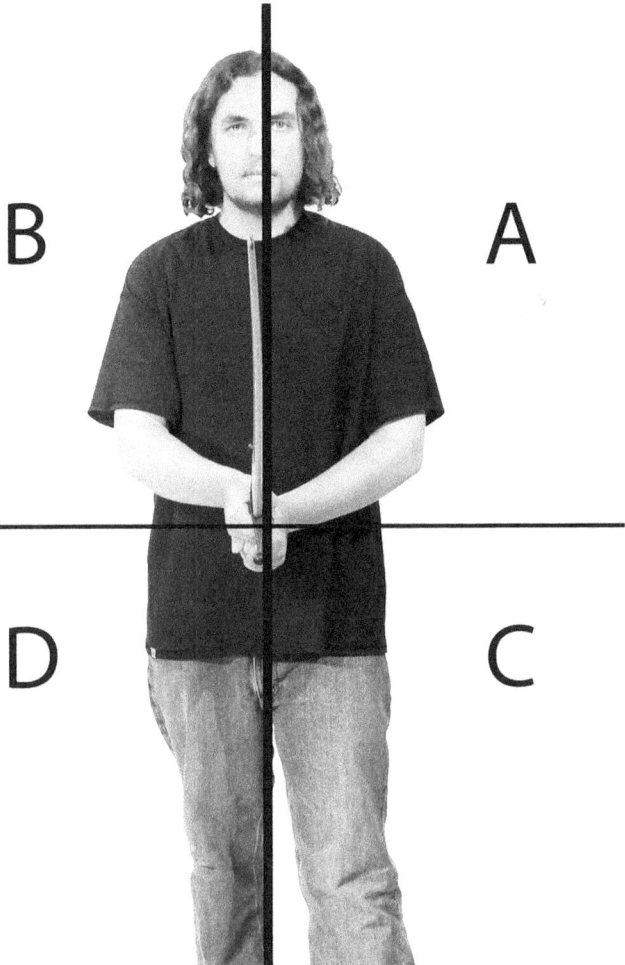

Figure 5.3 Four Zones

Note: Be careful not to twist your body away from your partner, thus losing your **fight-line** (also known as **line of direction**). Your back should be straight, and you should be looking forward at your partner. From this posture, you will be able to **transition** into any of the main guard positions.

24 WARDS AND GUARD POSITIONS

Figure 5.4 Base Stance

Stances

This section focuses on the five guard positions and their variations which I have found most useful in telling the physical story on stage. As you advance in your skill and knowledge, you will find that there are multiple variations of stances and guard positions.

The following stances and guard positions are important because they are the ready stances for receiving or delivering attacks. They give the fighter an advantage or provide protection. In performance, they physically tell the story about the fighter and their state of mind. Do they know what they are doing? Are they skilled fighters? Are they on the attack or are they staying completely defensive? These questions are answered by what kind of stance the performer is using, and how they use them.

Note on Right vs. Left-Handed: All stances are described for performers with right-hand dominance, if you or someone you are working with is left-hand dominant, reverse/mirror the postures.

General Points of Attention:

- Keep your elbows in and close to your body, be careful of "chicken wings", or your elbows lifted to shoulder level.
- Keep your shoulders relaxed. Try to avoid excess tension in your arms and shoulders as you want to be able to move your arms quickly and freely.
- Keep your knees bent and avoid locking your legs. There are many reasons to avoid locking your knees, however, in theatrical combat, being able to move in any direction at any time requires you to keep your knees bent and legs relaxed.
- Keep your hips, torso, and shoulders aligned toward your partner. Although there will be instances and exceptions where this is changed for certain postures.
- Keep your body upright and avoid hunching or leaning forward or backward.

Wards (Guards)

The beauty in sword work is in the transitioning of **Wards**, or guard positions. The shifting from one to the next allows the performer to block an attack and set the position of the **counterattack** in the same motion. When using wards effectively, a long-sword fight flows and obtains a dance-like quality. My goal is to overcome the misconceptions that broadswords are heavy bashing weapons that are hard to control. Instead, there is grace and amazing accuracy as the whole body becomes active and attuned with the sword.

The Historical Sources

Key: Historical Name [*alternative spelling*] (*English translation*)

In the late 14th-century Germany, Johannes Liechtenauer emphasized four primary wards for German long-sword use. Those were **Vom Tag** [Dach/Tach/Tage] (from the roof), **Ochs** (ox), **Pflug** (plow), and **Alber** (fool). Over the next century, Sigmund Ringeck, Hans Talhoffer, Peter von Danzig, Paulus Kal, Hans Medel von Salzburg, and Joachim Myer echoed these same wards in later works, wherein **Nebenhut** (near ward), a fifth ward, was added.

In the early 15th-century Italy, Fiore Dei Liberi writes of 12 wards for Italian long-sword use. Those were **Posta frontale ditta corona** (crown guard), **Posta di finestro** (window guard), **Posta breve** (short guard), **Tutta porta di ferro** (whole iron door), **Posta di donna** (woman's guard), **Posta di donna la sinestra** (woman's guard on the left), **Posta longa** (long guard), **Porta di ferro mezana** (middle iron door), **Dente di zenghiaro** (boar's tooth), **Posta di bicorno** (two-horned guard), **Posta di dente zenchiaro mezana** (middle boar's tooth guard), and the **Posta di Coda lunga** (long lying tail). These guards were repeated and adjusted by Filippo Valdi and Achille Marozzo over the next century.

Modern Guard Terminology for Theatrical Combat

As the art of theatrical combat grew and terminology became simplified, we have distilled all the many types of wards, postas, and guards down to a five simplified guard system:

- **The High Guard** – a guard at or above head level.
- **The Hanging Guard** – a guard at or above head level, with the blade held parallel with the ground or at an angle lower than the hilt.
- **The Middle Guard** – a guard in front of the body and below the shoulders, with the blade held with the tip directed up.
- **The Low Guard**– a guard in front of the body and below the shoulders, with the blade held with the tip directed down.
- **The Tail Guard** – a guard at the side of the body, at or below the waist, with the blade held with the hilt forward and the tip directed back.

The Five Primary Guards and Variations

The High Guard

The first ward is the **High Guard.** The high guard places the arms over the head and sword tip back about 45 degrees with either the left foot or right foot forward. This guard, known as **Vom Tag** in German and **Posta di falcone** (guard of the falcon) in Italian, is a perfect guard position for downward strikes, cuts, or blocks. Variations on this guard are **High Right/High Left**, the Italian **Posta frontale ditta corona** (crown

WARDS AND GUARD POSITIONS 27

Figure 5.5 High Guard

guard), **Posta di donna** (woman's guard), and **Posta di donna la sinestra** (woman's guard on the left side).

The Posture of the High Guard (Figure 5.5)

Stand with your feet shoulder width apart, left foot forward (this can also be done right foot forward), knees bent, weight equally distributed between your feet, shoulders, and hips forward, and sword lifted above the head with the blade tip back about 45 degrees, true edge up/forward. Make sure you do not block your vision, as your sword and arms should be above your eyeline.

Variations

The first variation of the high guard is the **High Right/High Left** (Figure 5.6)

Stand as you would for a high guard. In this position, the sword is lifted at or slightly above the shoulder, the hilt of the sword above the

Figure 5.6 High Right Guard

shoulder and not in front of the body, with the blade tip back about 45 degrees, true edge up and forward. The sword will be over the shoulder of whichever foot is back. For example, if your left foot is forward, the sword will be over your right shoulder. Your hips and shoulders should still face forward, making sure not to twist your body.

The second variation of the high guard is the Italian **Posta frontale ditta corona** (crown guard), which is held with the tip facing directly up and the hilt held at head level (Figure 5.7).

Stand as you would for a high guard, left foot forward, and sword lifted above the shoulder or head, with the blade tip pointing directly up. The hilt of the sword can be either at the chin level, or above the head, with the true edge facing directly left.

The third variations are the Italian guards of **Posta di donna** (woman's guard) (Figure 5.8).

Figure 5.7 Crown Guard

WARDS AND GUARD POSITIONS

Figure 5.8 Woman's Guard

Stand with your feet a little wider than shoulder width apart, left foot forward, knees bent, weight equally distributed between your feet. Your shoulders and hips facing forward, with the sword lifted over the right shoulder with the hilt on the right and the tip facing left behind you, elbows below your shoulder level (Figure 5.8a).

Posta di donna la sinestra is the same guard on the left side.

Stand with your feet a little wider than shoulder width apart, left foot forward, knees bent, weight equally distributed between your feet. Your shoulders and hips facing forward, with the sword lifted over the shoulder with the hilt on the left and the tip hanging down on the right side behind you (Figure 5.8b).

The Hanging Guard

The second ward is the **Hanging Guard.** The hanging guard, at or above head level, with the blade held parallel with the ground or at an angle with either the left foot or right foot forward. This guard, called **Ochs** (ox) in German and **Posta di finestro** (window guard) in Italian, is a perfect guard position for thrusts, strikes, cuts, or blocks. Variations include the **Hangort** (hanging point) and **Einhorn** (unicorn).

The Posture of the Hanging Guard (Figure 5.9)

Stand with your feet shoulder width apart, left foot forward, knees bent, and weight equally distributed between your feet. Your shoulders and hips turned slightly to the right, putting you in a slight profile forward. The sword lifted at or above the head on the right shoulder side with the blade tip facing forward. In this position, the true edge aims not upward or to the side, but away from the performer at about 45 degrees.

The position of the hands should be right hand on top, left hand on bottom. With this grip, you will find that your right forearm will be in alignment with the handle of the sword, and your right hand will be

Figure 5.9 Hanging Guard Right

palm out. Your left arm will cross your body, make sure you are not blocking your view with your arm, as your bicep should be below your chin line, and left palm facing in.

Left Side Hanging Guard (Figure 5.10)

Stand with your feet shoulder width apart, right foot forward, knees bent, and weight equally distributed between your feet. Your shoulders and hips turned to the left, putting you in a slight profile forward. The sword is lifted at or above the head on the left shoulder side with the blade tip facing forward. In this position, the true edge aims not upward or to the side, but away from the performer at about 45 degrees.

The position of the hands should be right hand on top, left hand on bottom. With this grip, you will find that your left forearm will be in alignment with the handle of the sword, and your left hand will be palm out. Your right arm will cross your body, make sure you are not blocking your view with your arm, as your bicep should be below your chin line, and right palm facing in.

Figure 5.10 Left Side Hanging Guard

Variations

The first variation of this guard is the **Hangort** (hanging point), with the point hanging down.

Stand as you would for hanging guard; the sword lifted at or above the head on the right shoulder side with the blade tip facing forward and alter the stance with a 45-degree angle downward of the blade.

Another variation on this guard is the **Einhorn** (unicorn), with the tip facing up.

Stand as you would for hanging guard; the sword lifted at or above the head on the right shoulder side with the blade tip facing forward and alter the stance by shifting the blade 45 degrees upward.

The Middle Guard

The third ward is the **Middle Guard.** The middle guard is in front of the body and below the shoulders, with the blade held with the tip directed up, with either the left foot or right foot forward. Known as **pflug** (plow) in German, this guard is a perfect guard position for thrusts, strikes, cuts, or blocks. The middle guard is commonly the "standard" **On Guard** stance for theatrical longsword. Variations include the Italian guards of **Posta di bicorno** (two-horned guard), **Posta breve** (short guard), and **Posta longa** (long guard).

The Posture of the Middle Guard (Figure 5.11)

Stand with your feet shoulder width apart, left foot forward, knees bent, and weight equally distributed between your feet. Your shoulders and hips should face forward in alignment with your partner. The sword held at about waist level, in front of your body, tip lifted at a 45-degree angle, true edge facing forward.

The position of the hands should be right hand on top, left hand on bottom. With this grip, the pommel of the sword will be to the right of your centerline, and your tip will be left of the centerline.

Left Side Middle Guard (Figure 5.12)

Stand with your feet shoulder width apart, right foot forward, knees bent, and weight equally distributed between your feet. Your shoulders and

34   WARDS AND GUARD POSITIONS

Figure 5.11 Middle Guard

Figure 5.12 Left Side Middle Guard

hips should face forward in alignment with your partner. The sword held at about waist level, in front of your body, tip lifted at about a 45-degree angle, true edge facing forward.

The position of the hands should be right hand on top, left hand on bottom. With this grip, the pommel of the sword will be to the left of your centerline, and your tip will be right of your centerline.

Variations on the Middle Guard

The first variation on the middle guard is **Posta breve** (short guard) (Figure 5.13).

Figure 5.13 Short Guard

Stand with your feet shoulder width apart, left foot forward, knees bent, and weight equally distributed between your feet. Your shoulders and hips should face forward in alignment with your partner. The sword held at about waist level, pulled in tight to your right hip, tip lifted at about a 45-degree angle, true edge facing down and forward. The position of the hands should be right hand on top, left hand on bottom. With this grip, the sword will be to the right of your centerline. The short guard can switch sides the same as the middle guard.

To switch to the left, step forward with the right foot and shift the sword to your left hip.

The second variation is the **Posta longa** (long guard) in Italian (Figure 5.14)

Stand with your feet twice shoulder width apart, right foot extended forward, knees bent, and weight equally distributed between your feet. Here, your back foot will have the heel raised. Your shoulders and hips should face forward in alignment with your partner. The sword held at

Figure 5.14 Long Guard

about chest level, pushed forward, still with a slight bend in the elbows, tip lifted at about a 30-degree angle, true edge facing forward. The position of the hands should be right hand on top, left hand on bottom. With this grip, the sword will line up with your centerline.

The long guard can switch sides the same as the short guard. To switch, take an extended step forward with the left foot, the sword should not shift.

The third variation is the **Posta di bicorno** (two-horned guard) (Figure 5.15)
Stand with your feet a bit wider than shoulder width apart, left foot forward, knees bent, and weight equally distributed between your feet. Your shoulders and hips should face forward in alignment with your partner. The sword held at shoulder level, pushed forward, still with a slight bend in the elbows, tip pointed forward, true edge facing down at 45 degrees. This grip centers the sword in line with the right shoulder.

The two-horned guard can switch sides the same as the short guard. To switch, step forward with the right foot, and the sword will shift to line up with the left shoulder.

Figure 5.15 Two-Horned Guard

The Low Guard

The fourth ward is the **Low Guard**. The low guard is in front of the body and below the shoulders, with the blade held with the tip directed down. In this guard, either leg may lead. The sword hilt rest toward whichever foot is back, as the tip breaks the centerline on the opposite side. Known as **Alber** (fool) in German and **Porta di ferro mezana** (middle iron door) in Italian, this guard is a highly effective guard for blocks and beats. Variations include the Italian guards of **Dente di zenghiaro** (boar's tooth) and **Posta di dente zenchiaro mezana** (middle boar's tooth).

The Posture of the Low Guard (Figure 5.16)

<u>Right Side</u> – Stand with your feet shoulder width apart, left foot forward, knees bent, and weight equally distributed between your feet. Your shoulders and hips should face forward in alignment with your partner. The sword held at about waist level, in front of your body, with the tip down at about a 45-degree angle, true edge facing down.

The position of the hands should be right hand on top, left hand on bottom. With this grip, the pommel of the sword will be to the right of your centerline, and your tip will be on the left of centerline (Figure 5.16a).

<u>Left Side</u> – Stand with your feet shoulder width apart, right foot forward, knees bent, and weight equally distributed between your feet. Your shoulders and hips should face forward in alignment with your partner. The sword held at about waist level, in front of your body, with the tip down at about a 45-degree angle, true edge facing down.

The position of the hands should be right hand on top, left hand on bottom. With this grip, the pommel of the sword will be to the left of your centerline, and your tip will be right of the centerline (Figure 5.16b).

Variations

The first variation of the low guard is **Dente di zenghiaro** (boar's tooth) in Italian.

Stand with your feet shoulder width apart, right foot forward, knees bent, and weight equally distributed between your feet. Your shoulders

WARDS AND GUARD POSITIONS 39

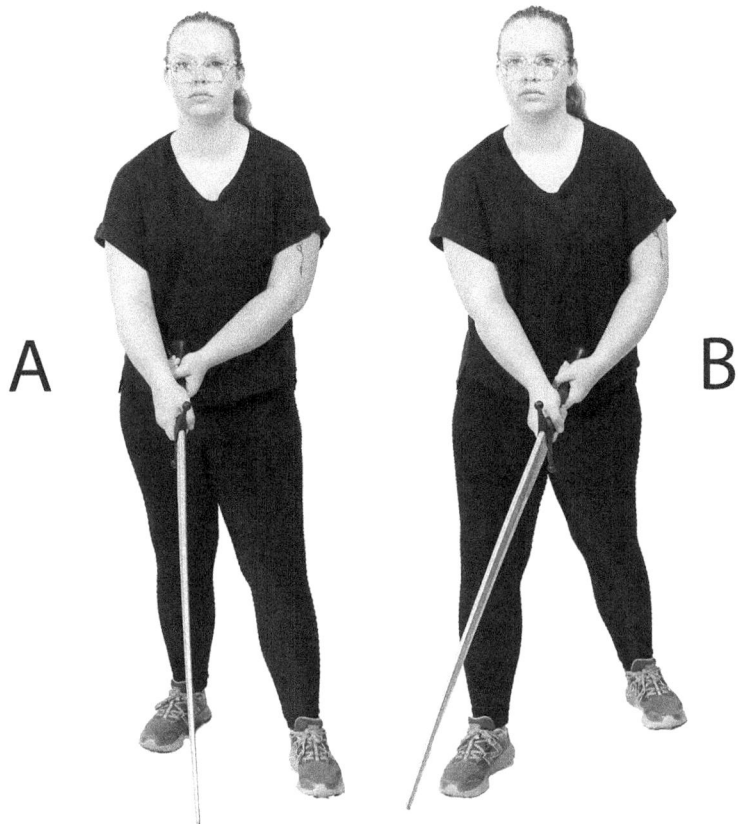

Figure 5.16 Low Guard

and hips should face forward in alignment with your partner. The sword held at about waist level, in front of and to the side of your left hip, tip down at about a 45-degree angle, true edge facing down.

The second variation is **Posta di dente zenchiaro mezana** (middle boar's tooth).

Stand with your feet shoulder width apart, right foot forward, knees bent, and weight shifted to your left leg. Your shoulders and hips opened out to the left, head still focusing forward toward your partner. The sword held at about waist level, in front of your hips, tip down at about a 45-degree angle, in line with your right leg, true edge facing down.

The Tail Guard

The fifth ward is the **Tail Guard**. The tail guard is at the side of the body, at or below the waist, with the sword held with the hilt forward and the blade directed back. This guard, called **Nebenhut** (near guard) in German and **Posta Coda Longa** (long tail) in Italian, provides strong raising actions for either attack or defense, and can be executed from either side of the body. The variation of this guard is the Italian **Tutta porta di ferro** (whole iron door).

The Posture of the Tail Guard (Figure 5.17)

<u>Right Side</u> – Stand with your feet shoulder width apart, left foot forward, knees bent, and weight equally distributed between your feet. Your shoulders and hips should face forward in alignment with your partner. The sword held slightly to the right hip, pommel facing forward, tip pointing back and down at a 45-degree angle, true edge facing down (Figure 5.17a).

The position of the hands should be right hand on top, left hand on bottom. With this grip, the pommel of the sword will point toward your partner, and the blade will be behind you, with the tip down at a 45-degree angle.

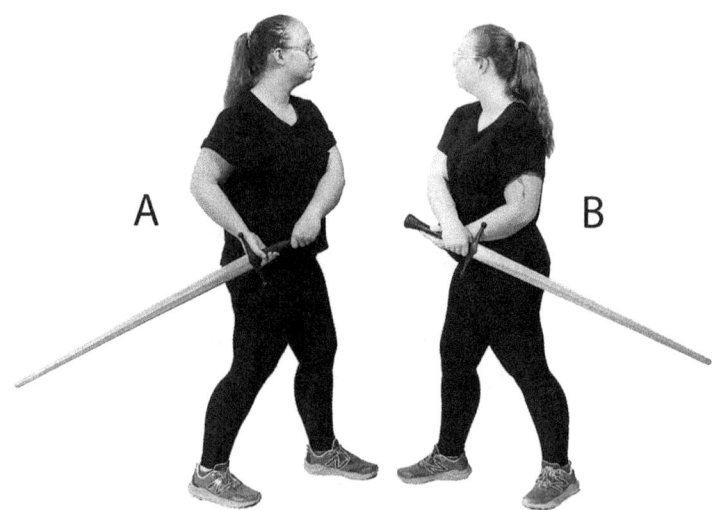

Figure 5.17 Tail Guard

Left Side – Stand with your feet shoulder width apart, right foot forward, knees bent, and weight equally distributed between your feet. Your shoulders and hips should face forward in alignment with your partner. The sword held slightly to the left hip, pommel facing forward, tip pointing back and down at a 45-degree angle, true edge facing down (Figure 5.17b).

The position of the hands should be right hand on top, left hand on bottom. You will find that your arms are crossed, and the grip of your left hand will have to be relaxed to hold the sword in this position. With this grip, the pommel of the sword will point toward your partner, and the blade will be behind you, with the tip down at a 45-degree angle.

Variation

The variation on this guard, called **Tutta porta di ferro** (whole iron door), brings the sword tip more out to the side and away from the body.

The posture of **Tutta porta di ferro**

Stand with your feet shoulder width apart, left foot forward, knees bent, and weight equally distributed between your feet. Your shoulders and hips should face forward in alignment with your partner. The sword held to the right hip with the tip down at a 45-degree angle, much the same as the tail guard, except with this position the sword will extend away from your body toward the right, instead of behind you.

Notes on Historical vs. Stage

An especially important note regarding safety: Historically, several guard positions have the sword tip aimed **on-line** at your opponent, and usually in the direction of their face. In theatrical combat, safety is the top priority. Therefore, never point a weapon or prop at your partner, and never in-line with their face. It is easy to move the tip **off-line**, outside of the body zone, and still maintain the **intention** of the guard stance.

Although some historical illustrations may make it look like the knee is bent or extended over the toes, be aware that you should never extend your knee over your toes or past them. Keep your knee above your ankle when in extended stances.

Open vs. Closed Guards

When talking about guards, we can refer to them as either being open or closed. An open guard is one where there are open lines of attack on the defender's body. Guards such as high guards and tail guards leave openings designed to draw an attack to the areas unprotected by the position.

Whereas a closed guard prevents any open lines of attack, thus providing better coverage and protection for the fighter.

Long vs. Short Guards

Guards can also be altered into long or short, also known as extended and close. A long guard is one which is extended away from the body as far as possible while still maintaining control, and a short guard is one where the sword is close to the body, tucked in closer than it would be in its natural guard state.

Short guards are extremely useful when in a group of fighters moving the same direction or in crowded fight scenes. Long guards are useful when you want to increase the distance between fighters, have a lot of space to fill on stage, or want to show a fighter who is either inexperienced or afraid.

Acting Notes

Always maintain your balance by keeping yourself centered. Keep your shoulders over your hips and do not overextend or lean forward or backward.

Keep your body relaxed. Do not allow extra tension in your shoulders or in your grip. Staying relaxed prevents fatigue and injuries.

Do not lock your knees. Again, stay relaxed, and keep a bend in both your knees and in your elbows. This prevents fatigue and injuries.

Do not point your sword at your partner's face, always aim slightly offline.

Make sure to pick the best guard position for the story and for the staging. Don't use a guard position that will block your face from the audience or the camera.

The use of extended or retracted guards can help tell the story you are performing. Extended guards can be aggressive, while retracted guards can give the impression of being more defensive.

Never use sharp or nontheatrical swords when doing stage combat. Always use proper equipment designed for theatrical combat.

Drills

Transition exercises for the guards:
Up & down right side:

1. Start in high guard – left foot forward
2. Shift down to high right
3. Shift into right hanging guard
4. Shift down to right middle guard
5. Shift into low right guard
6. Shift into right tail guard
7. Shift into low right guard
8. Shift up to right middle guard
9. Shift into right hanging guard
10. Shift up to high right
11. End in high guard

Up & down left side:

1. Start in high guard – right foot forward
2. Shift down to high left
3. Shift into left hanging guard
4. Shift down to left middle guard
5. Shift into low left guard
6. Shift into left tail guard
7. Shift into low left guard
8. Shift up to left middle guard
9. Shift into left hanging guard
10. Shift up to high left
11. End in high guard

Closing Comments

Do not get overwhelmed by all the different names and variations for the guard positions. Start by just focusing on the main five, and once those are mastered, look at adding in the variations. While having all those variations at your disposal is fun and can add more elements to your fight, you can manage a great dynamic fight with just the base guards. The guard positions are more than just stances, as we will see in the next few chapters how these positions provide the flow and dynamics to theatrical fights. Practicing these positions in combination with the footwork drills from the next chapter allows a performer to master their art and provide safe and exciting choreography to the story. One of the most important things to remember from this chapter is that one should always be relaxed and in control of the sword. Excess tension will only cause fatigue and inferior performance. Remember, we are here to tell a dynamic physical story in support of the plot.

6

FOOTWORK AND BODY DYNAMICS

The foundation for good movement during a choreography is proper footwork. Although broadsword and rapier share many of the same techniques when it comes to footwork, you will find that broadsword has a wider stance than the typical rapier or fencing stances and uses passes and wide steps with each action as well as the quick actions of advances, crosses, and slips. In this chapter, we are going to examine the fundamental movements of footwork in all directions, along with actions to remove yourself from the line of attack while maintaining your fighting line. Afterward, we will explore body dynamics and how it relates to telling of the physical story of the fight.

For the purposes of this chapter, all stances start from the basic on-guard posture (the middle guard) with the left foot leading (Figure 6.1).

46 FOOTWORK AND BODY DYNAMICS

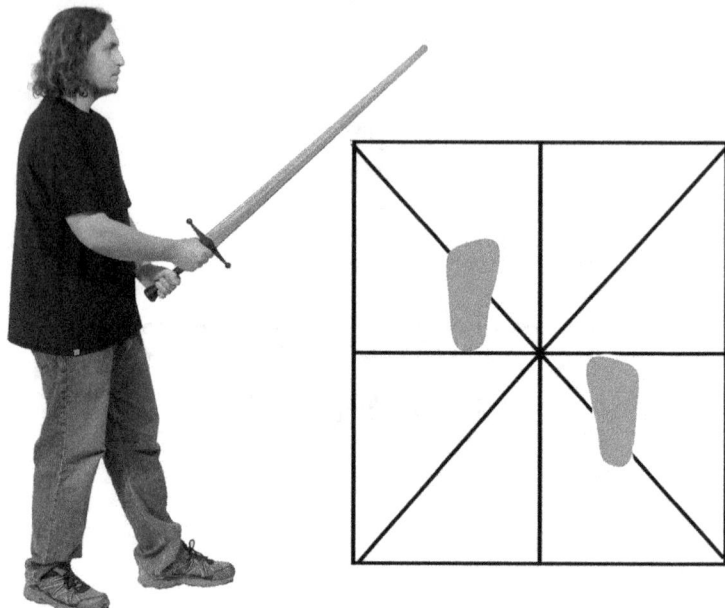

Figure 6.1 Opening Image of an Actor on Guard and a Footwork Pattern

The Basic Steps

Pass – A movement that takes the body in a straight line forward or backward by passing the foot and changing the lead foot (the foot in the front or forward position of the stance).

Pass Forward – Moving the right foot (lag foot), step forward with a full step in a straight line, left foot does not move forward. The left foot will have a small pivot as the right foot takes the lead position (Figure 6.2).

Pass Back – Moving the left foot (lead foot), step back a full step in a straight line, the right foot does not move back. The right foot will have a small pivot as it takes the lead position (Figure 6.3).

Traverse – Movement that takes the body in a straight line right or left and maintains the lead foot. These are used to either take the performer offline from an attack or used to maintain the fighting line during an attack.

Right – Move the right foot first, stepping to the right a full step. Follow this movement by stepping to the right with the left foot, one full

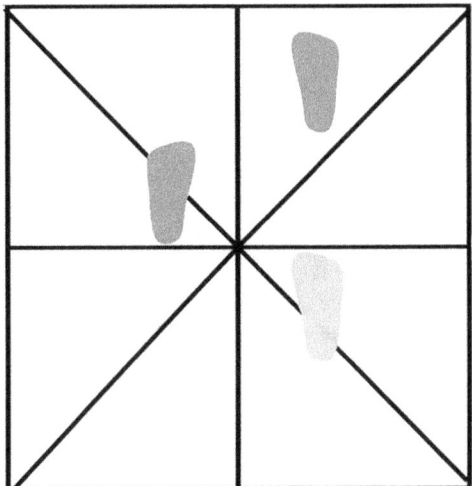

Figure 6.2 Pass Forward

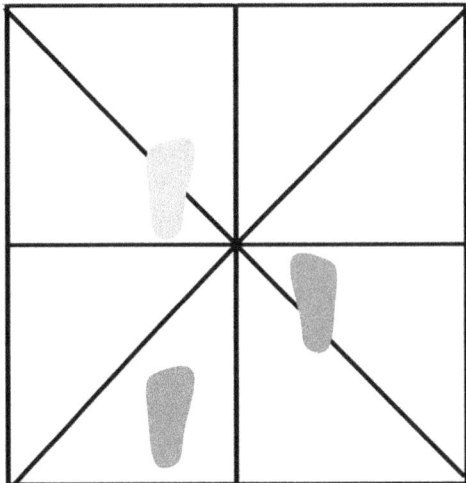

Figure 6.3 Pass Back

step. Your feet should still be in the original stance; however, you will be one step to the right in a straight line (Figure 6.4).

Left – Move the left foot first, stepping to the left a full step. Follow this movement by stepping to the left with the right foot, one full step.

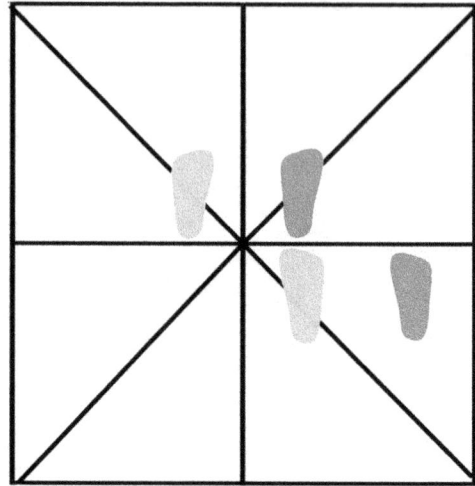

Figure 6.4 Traverse Right

Your feet should still be in the original stance; however, you will be one step to the left in a straight line (Figure 6.5).

Advance – Movement that takes the body forward along a straight line without crossing steps by transferring your weight to the lag foot, lift and move the lead foot forward one step. Shift the weight forward and move the lag leg forward the same distance (Figure 6.6).

Retreat – Movement that takes the body backward along a straight line without crossing steps by transferring your weight to the lead foot, lift and move the lag foot backward one step. Shift the weight back, and move the lead leg backward the same distance (Figure 6.7).

A note about advances and retreats: Although you are shifting your weight between your feet, you want to do your best not to lean forward or back during the action. Try to keep your torso centered and steady during these moves and not wobble back and forth.

Stepping Up the Game

Congratulations! You can now step forward and backward, and side to side. Now let us "step" up the game and start looking at movement along the diagonals at about 45 degrees.

FOOTWORK AND BODY DYNAMICS   49

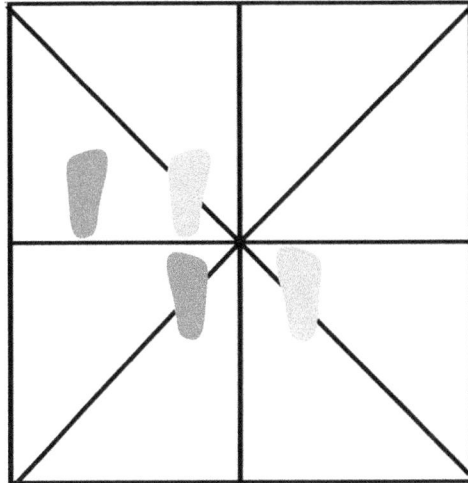

Figure 6.5 Traverse Left

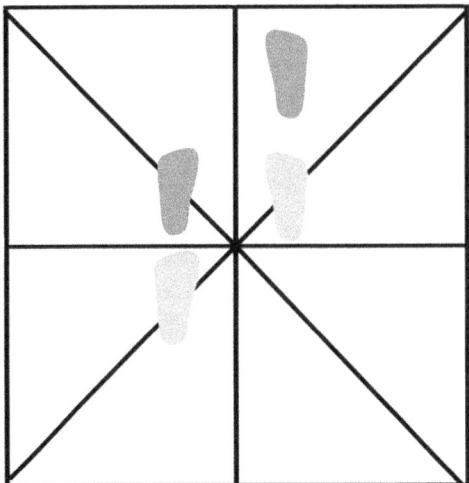

Figure 6.6 Advance

These actions will move your position and the direction you are facing, whereas advances and retreats will just move your position. The nonmoving foot will pivot on the ball of the foot – the area where the toes attach to the foot.

50 FOOTWORK AND BODY DYNAMICS

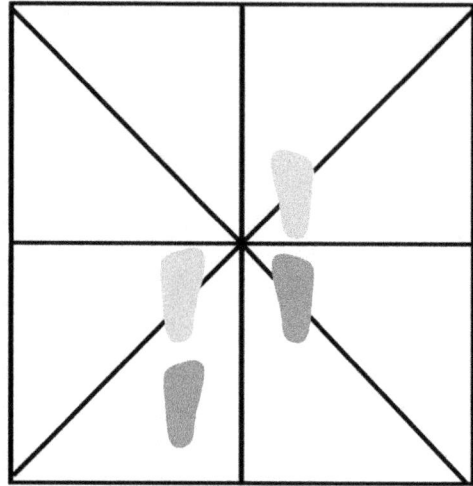

Figure 6.7 Retreat

Pass Forward Right – Moving the right foot (lag foot), step forward and to right with a full step in a diagonal line, about 45 degrees, making the right foot the lead foot. The left foot, now lag foot, will pivot on the ball of the foot to maintain the hips position with the body and balance. You should now be facing diagonally from your original starting position (Figure 6.8).

Pass Forward Left – Moving the right foot (lag foot), step forward and to left with a full step in a diagonal line, usually about 45 degrees, making the right foot the lead foot. The left foot, now lag foot, will pivot on the ball of the foot to maintain the hips position with the body and balance. You should now be facing diagonally from your original starting position (Figure 6.9).

Pass Back Right – Moving the left foot (lead foot), step back and to right with a full step in a diagonal line, usually about 45 degrees, making the right foot the lead foot. The right foot will pivot on the ball of the foot to maintain the hips position with the body and balance. You should now be facing diagonally from your original starting position (Figure 6.10).

Pass Back Left – Moving the left foot (lead foot), step back and to left with a full step in a diagonal line, usually about 45 degrees, making the

FOOTWORK AND BODY DYNAMICS   51

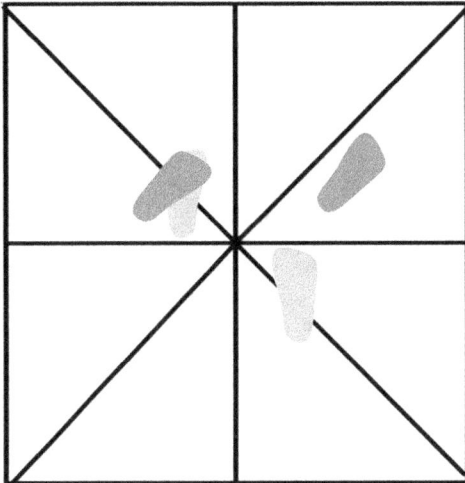

Figure 6.8 Pass Forward Right

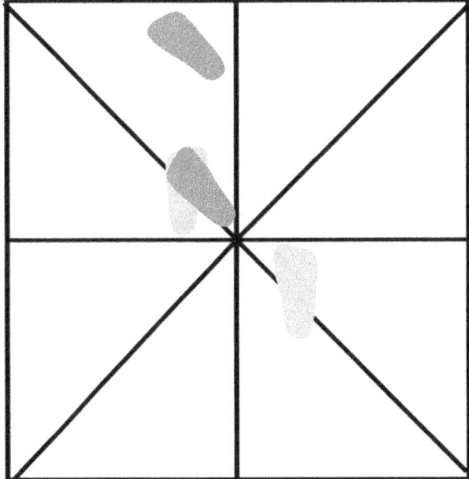

Figure 6.9 Pass Forward Left

right foot the lead foot. The right foot will pivot on the ball of the foot to maintain the hips position with the body and balance. You should now be facing diagonally from your original starting position (Figure 6.11).

52   FOOTWORK AND BODY DYNAMICS

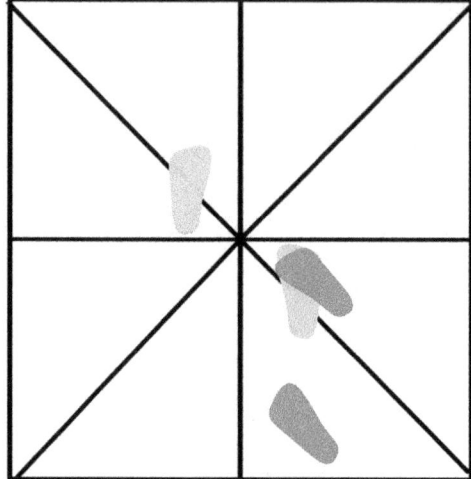

Figure 6.10 Pass Back Right

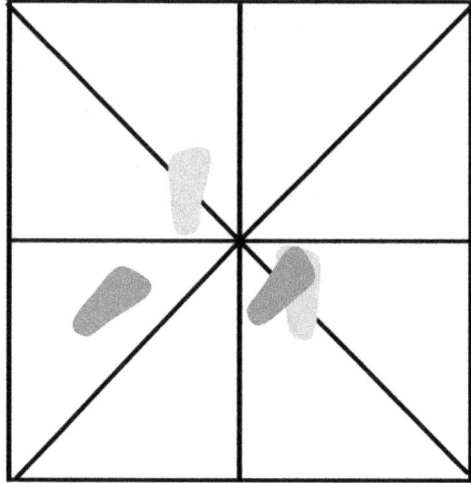

Figure 6.11 Pass Back Left

Advance Right – Move by stepping with the right foot (lag foot) diagonally forward toward your right at about 45 degrees. Once the foot is placed, move the left foot by stepping forward and to the right about 45 degrees. Your feet should end in the exact same position as the starting stance, hips and shoulders should still be facing forward (Figure 6.12).

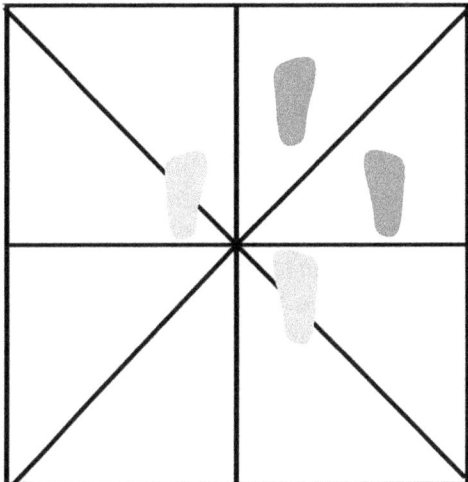

Figure 6.12 Advance Right

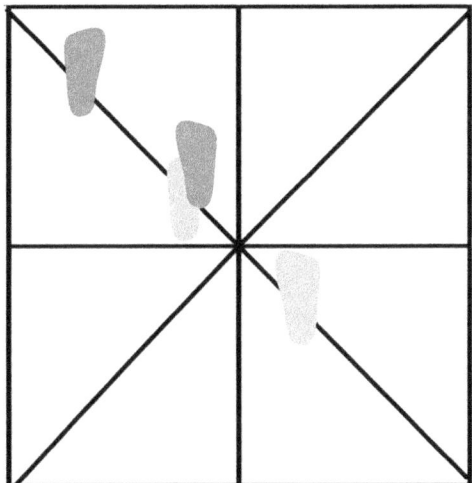

Figure 6.13 Advance Left

Advance Left – Move by stepping with the left foot (lead foot) diagonally forward toward your left at about 45 degrees. Once the foot is placed, move the right foot by stepping forward and to the left about 45 degrees. Your feet should end in the exact same position as the starting stance, hips and shoulders should still be facing forward (Figure 6.13).

Retreat Right – Move by stepping with the right foot (lag foot) diagonally back toward your right at about 45 degrees. Once the foot is placed, move the left foot by stepping back and to the right about 45 degrees. Your feet should end in the exact same position as the starting stance, hips and shoulders should still be facing forward (Figure 6.14).

Retreat Left – Move by stepping with the left foot (lead foot) diagonally back toward your left at about 45 degrees. Once the foot is placed, move the right foot by stepping back and to the left about 45 degrees. Your feet should end in the exact same position as the starting stance, hips and shoulders should still be facing forward (Figure 6.15).

Thwarts

Thwarts (also referred to as displacements) allow the performer to move the body offline from the attack. Thwarts are also used for offensive actions when a change of line is necessary. Here, the difference between a thwart and the passing step is the shift in balance, legs more open, and used as a defensive action (see Avoiding/Leaning below).

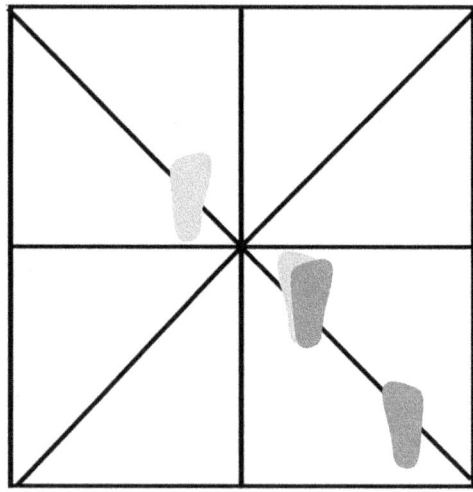

Figure 6.14 Retreat Right

FOOTWORK AND BODY DYNAMICS   55

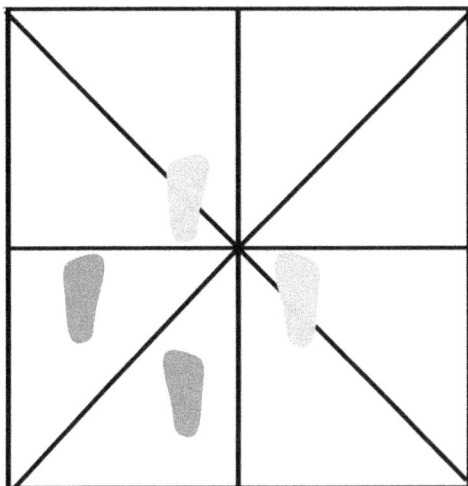

Figure 6.15 Retreat Left

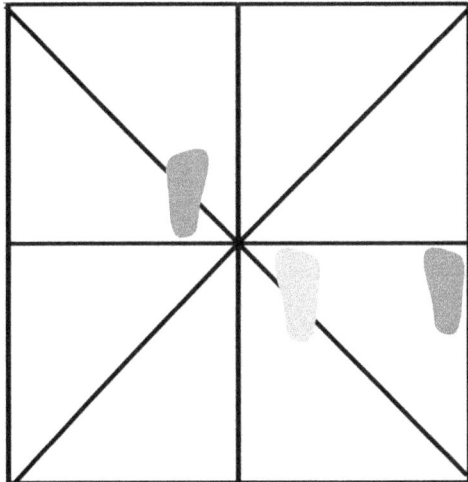

Figure 6.16 Thwart Right

Thwart Right – Move by stepping with the right foot (lag foot) toward your right (Figure 6.16).

Thwart Left – Move by stepping with the left foot (lead foot) toward your left (Figure 6.17).

56   FOOTWORK AND BODY DYNAMICS

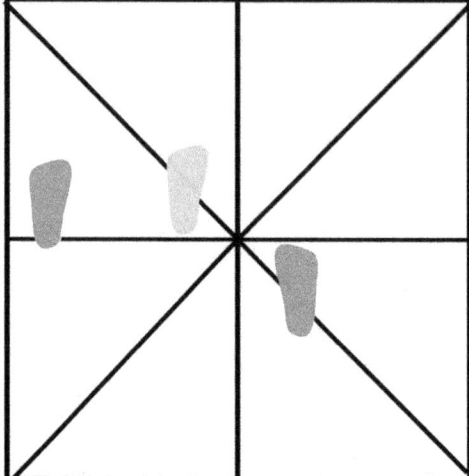

Figure 6.17 Thwart Left

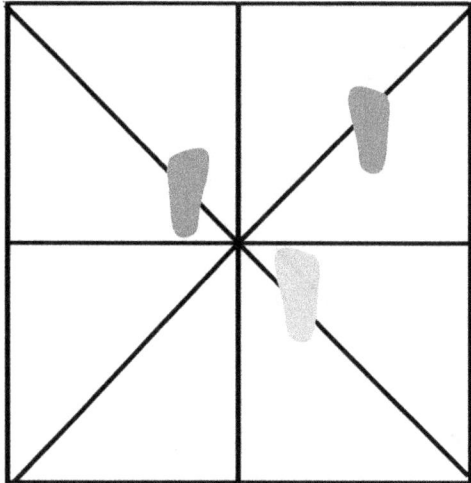

Figure 6.18 Thwart Forward Right

Thwart Forward Right – Move by stepping with the right foot (lag foot) diagonally forward toward your right at about 45 degrees (Figure 6.18).

FOOTWORK AND BODY DYNAMICS   57

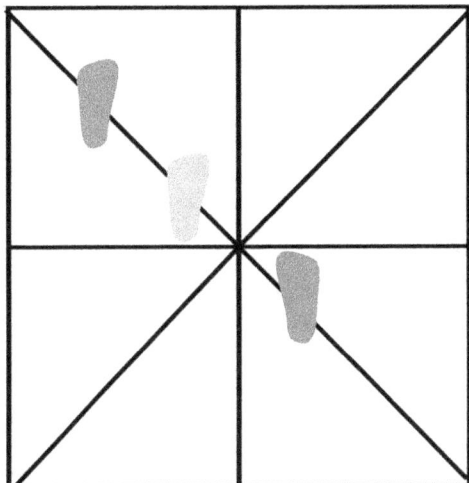

Figure 6.19 Thwart Forward Left

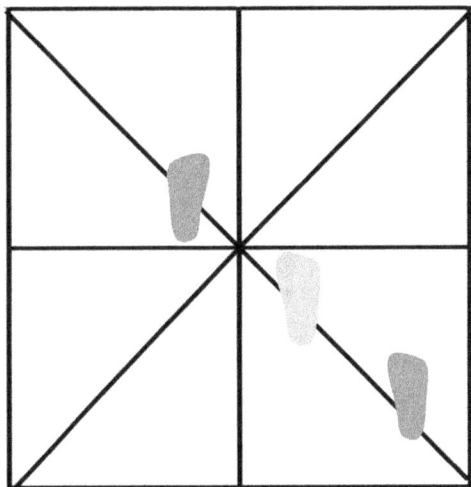

Figure 6.20 Thwart Back Right

Thwart Forward Left – Move by stepping with the left foot (lead foot) diagonally forward toward your left at about 45 degrees (Figure 6.19).

Thwart Back Right – Move by stepping with the right foot (lag foot) diagonally back toward your right at about 45 degrees (Figure 6.20).

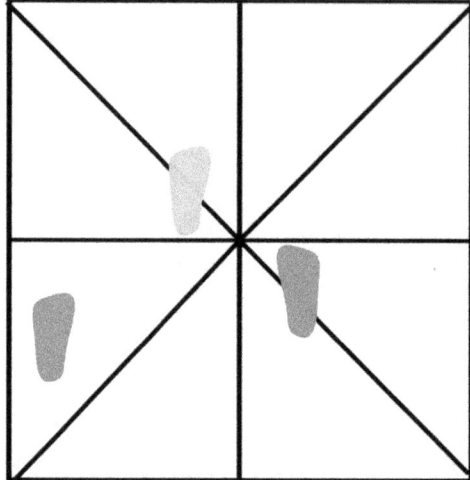

Figure 6.21 Thwart Back Left

Thwart Back Left – Move by stepping with the left foot (lead foot) diagonally back toward your left at about 45 degrees (Figure 6.21).

Keeping Everything in Line

Part of footwork is understanding the fight line. The **Fight Line**, also known as the line of direction or being squared up, is the path the combatants travel upon to maintain **engagement**. Imagine a line from you to your partner. This line is **engaged** when both of you have the same line, and are facing each other, squared up. You and your partner's hips and shoulders should face each other. When one individual shifts or moves that line away from their partner, they are off the fight line, and the one maintaining the fight line has the advantage. We will explore this concept more in the next chapter.

Transition exercises for the guards with footwork

1. Start in high guard – right foot forward
2. Shift down to high right with forward pass
3. Shift into right hanging guard with advance
4. Shift down to left middle guard with backward pass

5. Shift into low right guard with forward pass
6. Shift into right tail guard with retreat
7. Shift into low left guard with forward pass
8. Shift up to right middle guard with backward pass
9. Shift into right hanging guard with advance
10. Shift up to high right with retreat
11. End in high guard with forward pass

Up & down left side:

1. Start in high guard – left foot forward
2. Shift down to high left with forward pass
3. Shift into left hanging guard with advance
4. Shift down to left middle guard with backward pass
5. Shift into low left guard with forward pass
6. Shift into left tail guard with retreat
7. Shift into low left guard with forward pass
8. Shift up to left middle guard with backward pass
9. Shift into left hanging guard with advance
10. Shift up to high left with retreat
11. End in high guard with forward pass

Body Dynamics

Although footwork can add a level of excitement and realism to a choreography, we still need to continue telling the story of the fight with our upper body. This is where I see a lot of choreography fall short. There are many elements that can cause a choreography to lack energy such as actors' nerves, they are 100% focused on the blade work and not paying attention to their body work, or lacking movement where the two combatants are just facing each other, squared up, and swinging swords around. The body dynamics and intent of a fight, any fight, help accentuate the story being told and help the audience keep engaged with the fight.

To build these body dynamics, maintain your focus on your partner (or imaginary partner) and do not watch your feet. Stay in character and maintain your sword position and arms.

One of my top recommendations is as you are doing footwork drills, start adding in body dynamics, and let them become just as much as your habit as good strong footwork.

Body Engagement

In any physical work, core engagement is needed to keep your body in alignment and able to move in any direction. Always try to keep your upper torso straight and not hunched over (unless your character is injured, and that's a whole different game). Keep your shoulders relaxed and in line with your hips. Keep your lead foot pointed at your partner and keep a relaxed but firm grip on your sword. In the scene and in every action, maintain eye contact with your partner. This not only adds to the intensity of the scene but also keeps you both safe knowing that each of you is paying attention to each other and the actions.

Blade Awareness

Blade awareness goes beyond just what happens during the choreography. As a performer, you have to be aware of your sword at all times. This includes when you are wearing it on your side, if it's tucked into a belt, or in a sheath, you need to be aware of how far out the sword tip is behind you. This can become a challenge for some when it comes time to sit down while wearing a sword. Take the time to practice sitting while wearing a sword and discover what kind of adjustments you have to make. Also, pay attention to your sword when you are holding it in a noncombat manner. Where is your sword tip, what space around you may cause problems, are there a lot of people in a small space with swords out? These moments may not sound like much, but one wrong move, or someone not paying attention can cause injury, damage to a costume, or damage to a set. Another point to be aware of (yes, another pun) is when you are resting the sword over your shoulder. You need to be very aware of where your sword is pointing and who and what is around you. I have seen several actors turn around and put the sword into a wall or other set piece.

Avoiding/Leaning

As in any other style of fighting, the more variation of actions the more exciting a fight can be. Not every action needs a block. Sometimes avoiding an action or removing yourself from the attack can be just as exciting and dynamic as engaging with the blade. Leaning away from a cut as you thwart adds just a little bit more story to the action. But be careful not to overuse leans and start to add them into actions where you start creating bad habits.

Squats

Full-body squats are a great addition to a fight and can create a sense of levels and action. Things to be aware of while squatting away from a swipe is to make sure you maintain eye contact and that you bend at the knees and not the waist. And as mentioned before, be fully aware of where your sword is during the action. Can you use the squat to help prepare for the next action?

Jumps

Like squats, jumps are a great way to add excitement and levels to a fight. A tip to think about is to lift your knees on the vertical jump. It makes the jump easier and gives a visual sense of added height to the jump. When I choreograph a jump, I like to make sure the performer is holding on to both the handle and the blade near the tip. This provides for excellent blade control and awareness. When jumping either onto or off objects, always test items ahead of time for sturdiness and durability. The last thing you want is to jump on or off something and not support your launch or landing, which could cause injury.

Closing Comments

Footwork is key to creating exciting and dynamic fights. Take the time to practice and learn these skills. Bad footwork can make the fight look sloppy and create an unsafe environment for the performers and cast.

Another thing to be aware of is to check your performance area for any issues with the floor or ground. Lose boards, holes, or obstacles can all be problematic if not addressed at the beginning and avoided. As a director, try to give your fighters as much space as needed for a sword choreography, because unlike unarmed or knife, they need way more space. Not just to engage each other, but to also avoid other people and set pieces.

7

THE BASIC CUTS

Understanding the Offensive Actions of the Long-Sword

The beauty in broadsword choreography is the dominant offensive action of the **Cut**. A cut is an attack by a stroke or strike made with the edge of the blade. A secondary offensive action of the Long-Sword is the **Thrust**. A thrust is a pushing attack with the point of a blade. Other offensive actions which add to the beauty of choreography are the **draw cuts**, **swipes** and **slashes**, **pommel attacks**, **closing actions**, and **hilt bashes**, all of which we will examine in the advanced attacks chapter. This chapter will focus on and explain the various actions of the cut and thrust.

The Historical Sources

Key: Historical Name [*alternative spelling*] (*English translation*)

The early Italian systems described three methods of basic cuts (some of these terms are also from 16th-century manuscripts). In a high position, Fiore's two downward cuts from either the right or left were called **Fendenti** [Fendente], this cut was also listed by Vadi. From a low

Figure 7.1 Cuts

position, upward cuts from either the right or left were called **Sottani** [Sotano]. All horizontal cuts were called **Mezani** [Mezzane] by Fiore and called **Volanti** by Vadi.

These cuts could be divided further into Right-to-Left cuts called **Deritto** [Dritto, Dritti, Mandritto], and Left-to-Right cuts called **Riverso** [Riversi, Roversi]. Eventually, the diagonal cuts were called **Squalembrato** for descending diagonal cuts, and **Ridoppio** for rising diagonal cuts.

The German system described three methods of basic cuts: The downward cuts, either vertical or diagonal were called **Oberhau** (over cuts). The horizontal cuts, from either the left or the right, were called **Mittelhau** (middle cuts). Rising and upward cuts were called **Unterhau** (under cuts). The five Master Strikes of Liechtenauer, **Meisterhau**, will be covered later in Chapter 10.

Modern Theatrical Cuts

Horizontal Cuts to the High Line: Target Shoulder / Chest
Horizontal Cuts to the Low Line: Target Hip / Flank
Cuts on the Diagonals, both high and low lines
Cuts on the Verticals, both high and low lines

Notes on General Technique

How to **not** hit someone: understanding the technique of "Casting"

Unlike the martial arts we are portraying on stage, the techniques of stage combat are designed not to hit our partners. Instead, we create the illusion of force and violence. One of the techniques for creating this illusion of violence with swords is the use of **Casting**. Casting is the technique of directing or redirecting the energy of a weapon safely away from your partner while performing an attack.

Imagine a target out to the side of the actual target zone on the body. For this example, the target of the action will be our partners left shoulder. For the sword, the actual target will be 6 inches away from the shoulder. However, what we do not want to do is a technique called "pulling" the cut. That is, trying to stop and pull the cut back while attacking with energy directed at the body, as this will cause the blade to continue, and then whip back the other direction. What we want is to send all the energy forward, past our partner and not into them, and stop with a smooth action at our target. This is the same action as in casting a lure in fishing or throwing a frisbee. The illusion is completed when our partner parries the action.

Of Distance

Another technique for creating the illusion of violence on stage is the use of **Distance**. Distance is the space between the two performers during

THE BASIC CUTS

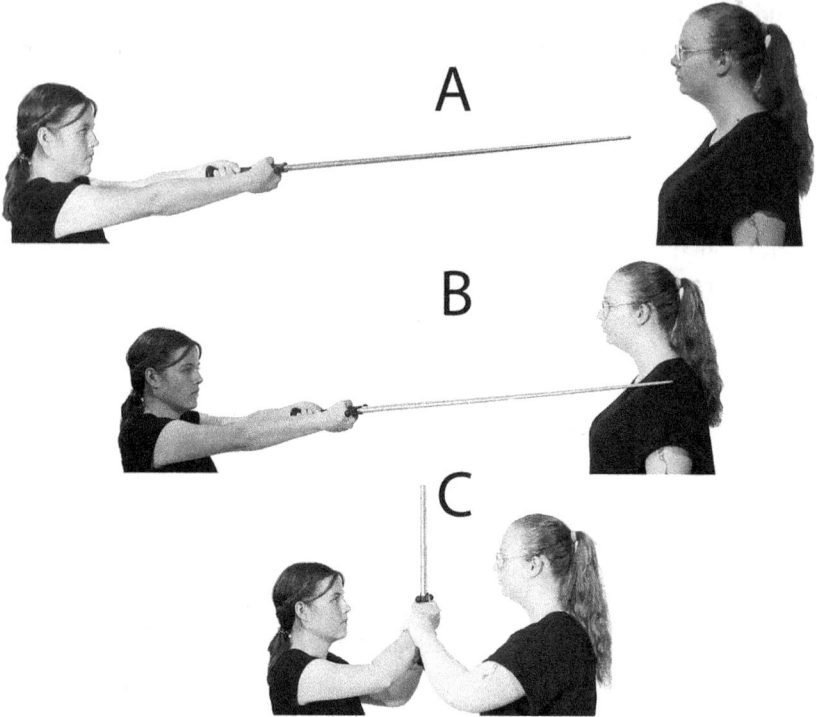

Figure 7.2 Distance

the choreography. The effective use of distance not only makes a staged fight more interesting and dynamic, but distance also helps maintain the safety for all the performers. When dealing with distance in sword fighting you have three measures, **Out of Distance, In Distance,** and **Closing Distance.** A good choreography should use all three measures effectively.

Out of Distance is when the distance between two performers prevents their weapon(s) from making physical contact with the other performer's body (Figure 7.2a).

In Distance is when the distance between two performers allows their weapon(s) to make physical contact with the other performer's body (Figure 7.2b).

Closing Distance is when the two performers both move in toward each other, closing the distance between them, so that they may physically grab or manipulate the other performer (Figure 7.2c).

The Method of Action

The **Method of Action** goes by many names, such as Action-Reaction-Action, Cue-Reaction-Action, or Preparation-Reaction-Action, to name a few. The method of action is the action of communicating with a partner during a choreography, while staying in character and maintaining a safe performance. We will go into detail about this in later chapters. Right now, I just want you to remember that the fight choreography is a conversation between two performers telling a story, not just two characters on stage beating each other up.

The Composition of a Cut

A longsword cut is an attack with the edge of the blade. Understanding and employing proper technique not only improves the quality of the performance but also helps prevent physical injury and strain.

The Beginning Actions: Although all actions can be initiated either at the core or at the feet, we are going to look at how cuts are visually initiated from one of three locations of the arms:

The Shoulders – A cut initiated from the shoulders will appear powerful, but the action of the attack will be slow. This attack is great when wanting to deliver powerful final attacks, when dealing with rage, or wanting to show the character as unskilled with a larger or heavy weapon.

The Elbows – A cut initiated from the elbows will appear quick, with precision, and show skill with a sword. Actions initiated from the elbows make up many of the techniques used on stage.

The Wrists – A cut initiated from the wrist will lack strength but will be a quick action. Actions initiated from the wrist are small cuts to the body or beats to the opposing weapon. Character use of these actions usually shows great skill with a sword.

Although the cut may initiate in one of these locations, proper technique will utilize the entire arm and body, and good choreography will contain cuts from all three initiators.

The Middle Action: The action of the cut itself is an arcing action. A cut may be a full circle or just a quick strike, the path depending on its starting position and its destination.

The Quick Cut – This cut goes straight from the guard position to the target. Guards that usually employ the quick strike are the Tail and High Guards.

The Circular Cut – This cut builds energy by traveling in a circle to its intended target. Guards that usually employ the circular strike are the Low, Middle, and Hanging Guards.

The Chop Cut – This cut builds energy by lifting or removing the sword from its guard location in the opposite direction of the target and then follows the same path back toward the target. A Middle Guard, or even a Low Guard, can be quickly lifted into a High Guard before being brought down to strike a head cut.

The Ending Action: At the end of the action (unblocked), you will find that you are back in a guard position.

An example would be that a quick strike from a high guard could end in either a low guard or a tail guard.

If blocked, you should find yourself fully cast at the intended target, having met your partner's block.

This does not account for actions such as interruptions, beats, displacements, or closing actions. All of which will be covered in latter chapters.

Use the True Edge

As mentioned back in Chapter 3, when talking about the parts of a sword, the True Edge is the edge of the blade on the same side as your knuckles. And while some advanced actions may use the flat and/or false edge of the blade, most of your actions will be true edge focused, thus you will be attacking with the true edge of the blade.

The Basic Cuts of the Long-Sword

Horizontal Cuts to the High Line

The High Lines, as illustrated in Figure 7.3a, are the target areas of the body above the waist. Targets can include the stomach, the chest, the shoulders, and the head. Horizontal attacks to the high line include the **Cut to the Right Shoulder** and the **Cut the Left Shoulder.** Other

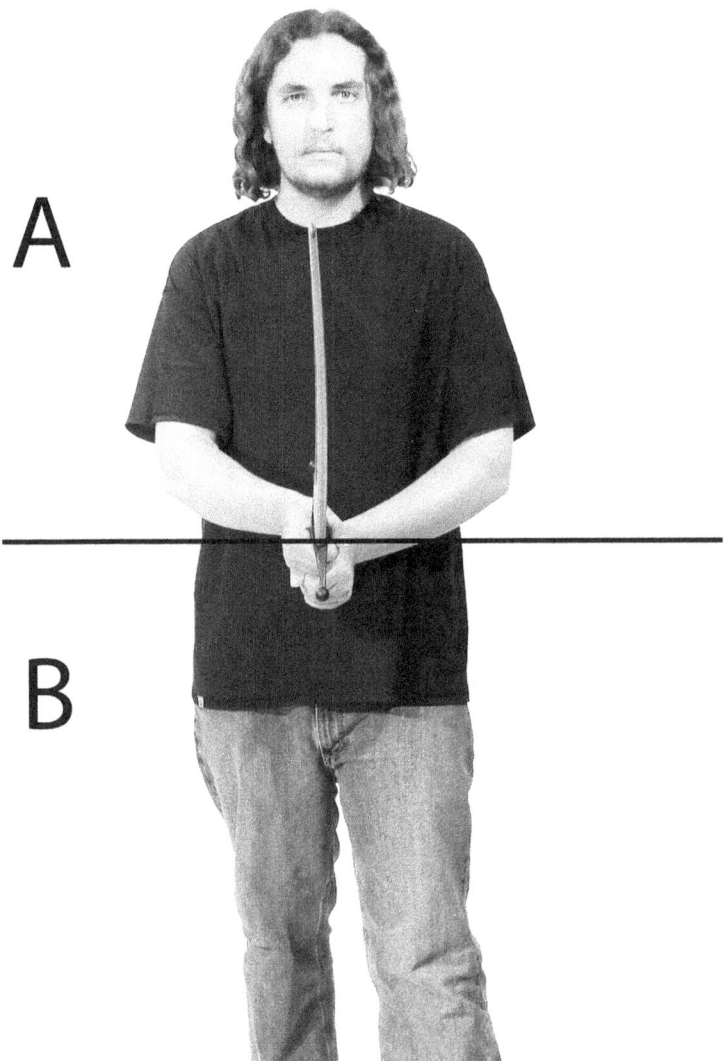

Figure 7.3 Lines of Attack

high-line horizontal attacks include the belly swipes, diagonal swipes, and horizontal head swipes. **Swipes** are cutting actions that pass through the target area without making contact and are not blocked but are avoided. Swipes are covered later in Chapter 10.

The Action of the Horizontal Cut to the Right Shoulder

From the middle guard with right foot forward, perform a circler cut with your sword, clockwise, from your right to your left, sending your blades energy behind the right shoulder target of your partner (Figure 7.4a).

Pass forward with the left foot, as your sword moves toward your partner, not before. If your partner is at the "12 o'clock" position, as your sword moves forward from the "9 o'clock" position you pass forward (Figure 7.4b).

This can also be done with the left foot forward; you would just advance forward instead of pass forward.

The Action of the Horizontal Cut to the Left Shoulder

From the middle guard with right foot forward, perform a circler cut with your sword, counterclockwise, from your left to your right, sending your blades energy behind the left shoulder target of your partner (Figure 7.5a).

Advance forward, as your sword moves toward your partner, not before. If your partner is at the "12 o'clock" position, as your sword moves forward from the "3 o'clock" position you advance forward (Figure 7.5b).

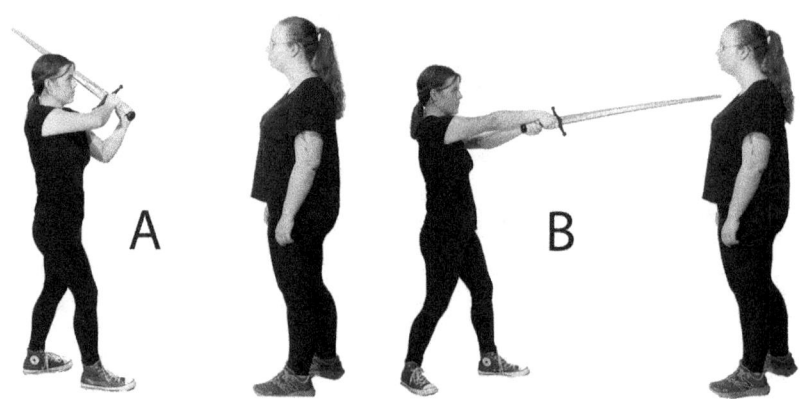

Figure 7.4 Cut to Right Shoulder

THE BASIC CUTS   71

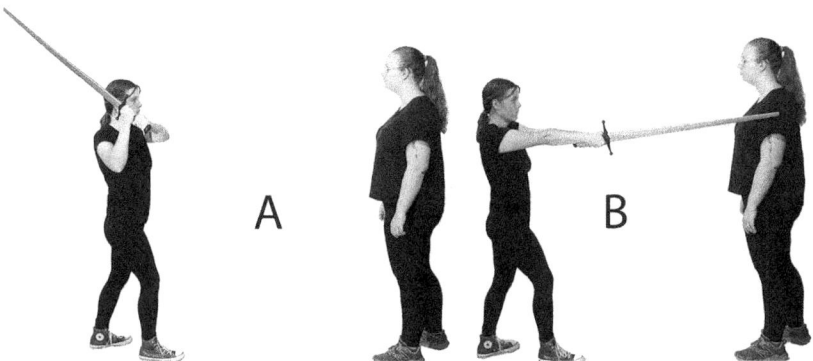

Figure 7.5 Cut to Left Shoulder

This can also be done with the left foot forward. If your partner is at the "12 o'clock" position, as your sword moves forward from the "3 o'clock" position you pass forward.

Variations: The Actions of the Horizontal Cut to a High Line from Various Guards

High Guard – From the high guard with the right foot forward, perform a quick cut to the shoulder target. Make sure to send your blades energy behind the target, passing forward for an attack to the right shoulder, or advancing forward for an attack to the left shoulder (opposite for left foot forward).

This may be altered into a circular cut if you are in a high right or high left and attacking the opposite side target. Footwork will remain as above.

Hanging Guard – From the hanging guard on the right side, perform a circular cut to the shoulder target. Make sure to send your blades energy behind the target, advancing forward for an attack to the right shoulder, or pass forward for an attack to the left shoulder.

From the hanging guard on the left side, perform a circular cut to the shoulder target. Make sure to send your blades energy behind the target, pass forward for an attack to the right shoulder, or advance forward for an attack to the left shoulder.

Low Guard – From the low guard position with the right foot forward, perform a circular cut to the shoulder target. Make sure to send your blades energy behind the target, passing forward for an attack to the right shoulder, or advancing forward for an attack to the left shoulder (opposite for left foot forward).

Tail Guard – From the tail guard on the right side perform a quick cut to the left shoulder target, or a circular cut to the right shoulder target. Make sure to send your blades energy behind the target. In this guard you will pass forward for an attack to the left shoulder or advancing forward for an attack to the right shoulder. This will be reversed for a tail guard on the left side.

Horizontal Cuts to the Low Line

The Low Lines, as illustrated in Figure 7.3b, are the target areas of the body at or below the waist. Targets can include the hips, legs, flank, and groin. Horizontal attacks to the low line include the **Cut to the Right Hip** and the **Cut the Left Hip.** Other low-line horizontal attacks include the leg swipes. Swipes are covered later in Chapter 10.

The Action of the Horizontal Cut to the Right Hip

From the middle guard with right foot forward, perform a circler cut with your sword, clockwise, from your right to your left, sending your blades energy behind the right hip target of your partner (Figure 7.6a).

Cross forward with the left foot, as your sword moves toward your partner, not before. If your partner is at the "12 o'clock" position, as your sword moves forward from the "9 o'clock" position you pass forward (Figure 7.6b).

This can also be done with the left foot forward. If your partner is at the "12 o'clock" position, as your sword moves forward from the "9 o'clock" position you advance forward.

Figure 7.6 Cut to the Right Hip

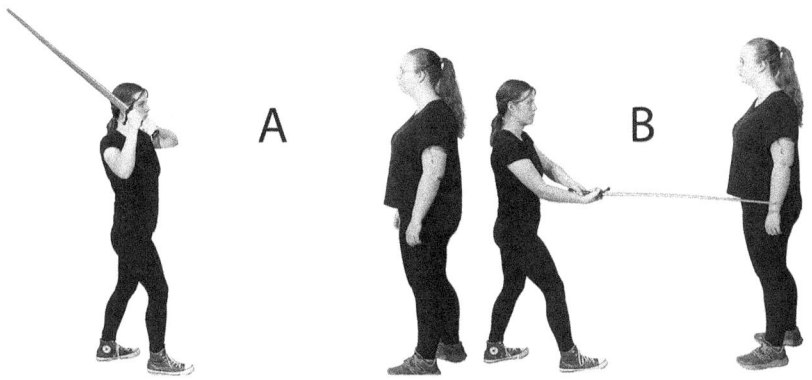

Figure 7.7 Cut to the Left Hip

The Action of the Horizontal Cut to the Left Hip

From the middle guard with right foot forward, perform a circler cut with your sword, counterclockwise, from your left to your right, sending your blades energy behind the left hip target of your partner (Figure 7.7a).

Advance forward, as your sword moves toward your partner, not before. If your partner is at the "12 o'clock" position, as your sword moves forward from the "3 o'clock" position you advance forward (Figure 7.7b).

This can also be done with the left foot forward. If your partner is at the "12 o'clock" position, as your sword moves forward from the "3 o'clock" position you pass forward.

Variations: The Actions of the Horizontal Cut to a Low Line from Various Guards

High Guard – From the high guard with the right foot forward, perform a quick cut to the hip target. Make sure to send your blades energy behind the target, passing forward for an attack to the right hip, or advancing forward for an attack to the left hip (opposite for left foot forward).

This may be altered into a circular cut if you are in a high right or high left and attacking the opposite side target. Footwork will remain as above.

Hanging Guard – From the hanging guard on the right side, perform a circular cut to the hip target. Make sure to send your blades energy behind the target, advancing forward for an attack to the right hip, or pass forward for an attack to the left hip.

From the hanging guard on the left side, perform a circular cut to the hip target. Make sure to send your blades energy behind the target, pass forward for an attack to the right hip, or advance forward for an attack to the left hip.

Low Guard – From the low guard position with the right foot forward, perform a circular cut to the hip target. Make sure to send your blades energy behind the target, passing forward for an attack to the right hip, or advancing forward for an attack to the left hip (opposite for left foot forward).

Tail Guard – From the tail guard on the right side perform a quick cut to the left hip target, or a circular cut to the right hip target. Make sure to send your blades energy behind the target. In this guard, you will pass forward for an attack to the left hip or advancing forward for an attack to the right hip. This will be reversed for a tail guard on the left side.

Cuts on the Diagonals

Cuts on the diagonals follow the same starting actions as the cuts on the horizontal. The main difference is instead of coming into the target flat, they come in at an angle appropriate to the target. The cuts are still cast in the same way as above, focusing on using the true edge, and the target is still the hips and shoulders.

The Action of the Diagonal Cut to the Right & Left Shoulder

Right Shoulder – From the middle guard with right foot forward, perform a circler cut with your sword, clockwise, from your right to your left, sending your blades energy behind the right shoulder target of your partner (Figure 7.8a). Pass forward with the left foot, as your sword moves toward your partner (Figure 7.8b).

Left Shoulder – From the middle guard with right foot forward, perform a circler cut with your sword, counterclockwise, from your left to your right, sending your blades energy behind the left shoulder target of your partner (Figure 7.8c). Advance forward, as your sword moves toward your partner (Figure 7.8d).

The Action of the Diagonal Cut to the Right & Left Hip

Right Hip – From the middle guard with right foot forward, perform a circler cut with your sword, clockwise, from your right to your left, sending your blades energy behind the right hip target of your partner. Cross forward with the left foot, as your sword moves toward your partner. Note – your left wrist will be crossed under your right wrist at the end of this cut, so make sure you are cutting with your true edge of the sword.

Left Hip – From the middle guard with right foot forward, perform a circler cut with your sword, counterclockwise, from your left to your right, sending your blades energy behind the left hip target of your partner. Advance forward, as your sword moves toward your partner.

76 THE BASIC CUTS

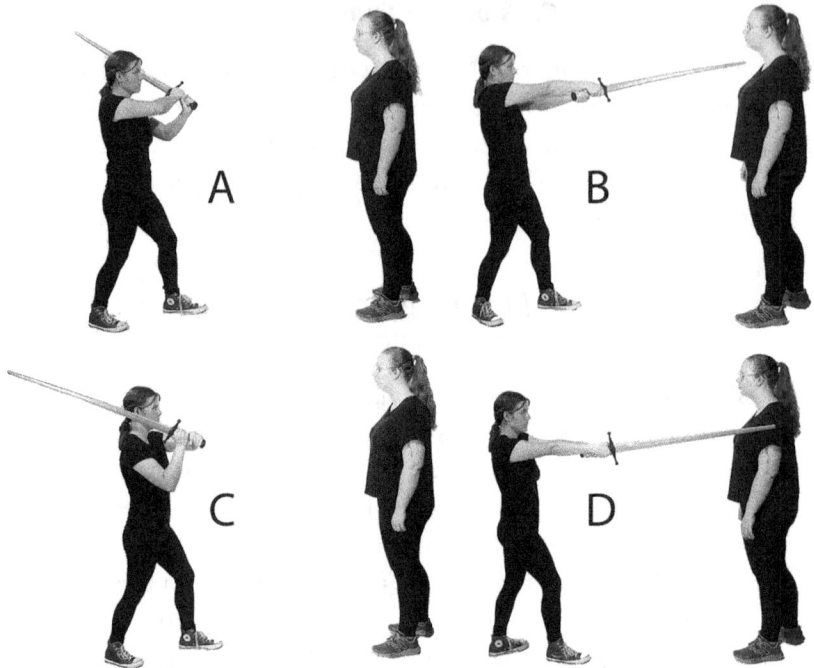

Figure 7.8 Diagonal Cuts to the Shoulders

Cuts on the Verticals

Cuts on the vertical line down are a very common action; however, cuts on the vertical line up are a little less common and will not be explored here in this section, and we will only focus on the two downward cuts to your partner's shoulders.

The Action of the Rolling Vertical Cut Down to the "Head"

In theatrical combat, we never want to direct our weapon at our partner's head. We will always take it offline, and our actual "target" is to either the right or left shoulder.

Like all cuts in this chapter, this action is cast beyond our partner, and no energy is directed down into their body.

Right Side Roll, Left Side Target – From the middle guard with left foot forward, perform a circler cut, also known as a **Moulinet**, with your sword from your right side. To perform this, drop the tip of your sword down to your right, and roll it backward away from your partner, bringing the tip up behind you (Figure 7.9a), then down to your target of your partners left shoulder zone as you extend your arms and cast your energy (Figure 7.9b). The trick here is to not let your hilt & hands go behind your body. Cross forward, as your sword moves toward your partner. (Note: In the photo, the sword looks very close to their partners head, it is not. It is a good 9–12 inches away, and directly over their left shoulder.)

Left Side Roll, Right Side Target – From the middle guard with right foot forward perform a circler cut with your sword from your left side (Figure 7.10a). To perform this, drop the tip of your sword down to your left, and roll it backward away from your partner, bringing the tip up behind you, then down to your target of your partners right shoulder zone as you extend your arms and cast your energy (Figure 7.10b).

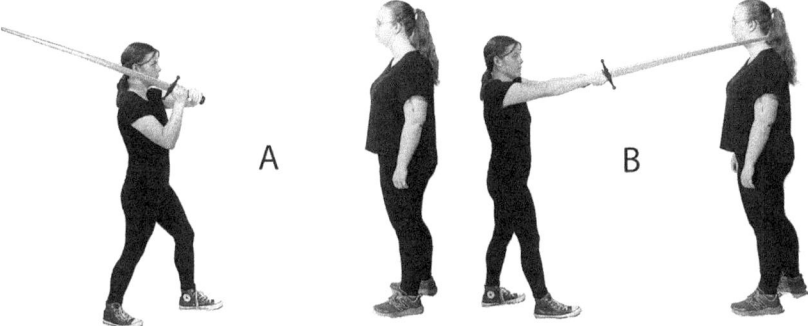

Figure 7.9 Head Cut to the Left Shoulder

Figure 7.10 Head Cut to the Right Shoulder

The trick here is to not let your hilt & hands go behind your body. Cross forward with the left foot, as your sword moves toward your partner.

Nonrolling Attacks – Both of these actions can be done without the roll, especially if you are in high guard, by simply dropping your attack down to the should of your partner. If you are in high center guard, start by dropping your hands and guard toward your target shoulder, then extend your tip, casting your energy at the target.

If you are in High-Right or High-Left, target the same side – for example, if you are in High-Right you will attack the left shoulder, and High-Left will attack the right shoulder.

Point Attacks and Thrusts

In this section, we will look at the basic point attacks and thrusts. Unlike later weapons like the rapier, lunges are not a part of broadsword, but that's not to say point attacks were not used. They were very common and can add some nice dynamics to a choreography. In Chapter 10, we will look at other more advanced point attacks, but for now, we will cover the basics from various guard positions.

On-Line vs Off-Line

On-line refers to attacks made directly toward the partners body, while **Off-line** refers to attacks aimed at targets away from the body. If we were thrusting our sword forward and we were aiming at our partners belly, and at full extension, we would hit their belly if they do not block or move, that is on-line. However, we can do the same action off-line by moving our target just outside the body by 3–4 inches. So that if our partner does not move or block, they would not get hurt. I go into more detail of using on- or off-line attacks in later in this book.

Although point attacks can target various spots on a partner's body, except the face, we are going to focus all our attacks on the center mass of our partner but keep everything off-line.

THE BASIC CUTS   79

Figure 7.11 Point Attacks

The Actions of Straight Point Attacks from Various Guards

High Guard – From the high guard with the right foot forward, perform a cut down, when you are at about 45 degrees forward, you will pull your sword in toward your center, then push it forward toward your partner, aiming either to the right or left of their body, passing forward for an attack to their right, or advancing forward for an attack to their left (opposite for left foot forward).

A variation of this is to take away the cut, and just drop from a high guard into a middle guard position.

Hanging Guard – From the hanging guard on the right side, point your tip at your target on your partners right or left side, then extend your sword forward toward the target, following a straight path. Make sure to send your blades energy behind the target, pass forward for an attack to their left, or advancing forward for an attack to their right. For the hanging guard on the left side, just mirror the actions above.

Middle Guard – From the middle guard position with the right foot forward, point your tip at your target on your partners right or left side, then push your sword forward toward the target, following a straight path. Make sure to send your blades energy behind the target, pass forward for an attack to their right, or advancing forward for an attack to their left. For the middle guard with left foot forward, just mirror the actions above.

Low Guard – From the low guard position with the right foot forward, start by lifting your sword tip and pointing it at your target on your partners right or left side, then push your sword forward toward the target, following a straight path. Make sure to send your blades energy behind the target, pass forward for an attack to their right, or advancing forward for an attack to their left. For the low guard with left foot forward, just mirror the actions above.

Tail Guard – From the tail guard on the right side perform a quick shift from tail to short guard (posta breve) on your left hip, then extend your sword and pointing it at your target on your partners right or left side, then push your sword forward toward the target, following a straight path. Make sure to send your blades energy behind the target, pass forward for an attack to their left, or advancing forward for an attack to their right. For the tail guard on the left, just mirror the actions above.

Cutting Drills

Cutting drills are a great way to practice your form and develop a smooth flow to your actions. Even Joachim Meyer in his 1570 book (remember from Chapter 2, the one with the ridiculously long name) had a section dedicated to cutting drills, which we will explore in detail further below.

Horizontal and Diagonal Cutting Drill with Passing Footwork

This drill can be done starting from the various guard positions and can be done in any order you would like. Here, we start in high right guard and just work around the body. Remember to cast your cut at the end of your action.

1. Start in high right guard, right foot forward – cut to partners right shoulder with passing step.
2. Cut to left shoulder with forward pass
3. Cut to right hip with forward pass

4. Cut to left hip with forward pass
5. Roll the cut up for vertical cut to head on their right shoulder side with forward pass

Now repeat this drill from a different guard until you have gone through all the guards and cuts, then switch to diagonal cuts from all guard positions. You can even mix it up by switching between horizontal to diagonal.

Meyer's Drill

The above image may not make a lot of sense right now, but once you understand the process, this will become quite easy to follow. Starting from the outside perimeter inward, follow along the numbers 1 through 4 for the order of attack. The first cut goes to the left shoulder of your partner (1), the second strike goes to the right hip (2), the third strike goes to the left hip (3), and the fourth and final strike goes to the right shoulder (4). On the second round, you would start with a cut to the left hip, third round you start with a cut to the right shoulder, and fourth and final round you start with a cut to the right hip. For a variation, you can start with the inside perimeter and work your way out.

Figure 7.12 Meyer's Drill

Cut-Through Drill – Finding the Flow

In this drill, the goal is to start in one guard position, perform a cut, allow it to pass through the target, and end the action in a guard position.

Example: Starting in a high right guard, left foot forward, cut toward your partner's left shoulder. If you are practicing this with a physical partner, they should be far out of distance and matching your movement. As your cut passes through the target, end your action in a low guard position with your right foot forward. From there, roll your cut up and around to attack the right hip, step forward with your left foot, and end your action in a right-hanging guard.

Continue these actions finding all the different variations of guards and cuts, just make sure to move forward with each action and find the flow.

Closing Comments

Just as before with the guard positions, do not become overwhelmed by all the different names and variations for the cuts. Take the time to learn the basics, then slowly add in the variations. You can even make a simple choreography with the cutting drills once you add in the blocks and parries from the next chapter. One thing to pay attention to is the use of your body during the actions. Make sure you are always in proper alignment during your cuts, and that you are stepping with the correct foot forward, and not leaning forward with your upper body at the end of the action. You want to keep your body aligned and prevent your body from twisting, which usually results from stepping with the wrong foot. Remember, you want to step with the same foot as the side you are cutting toward and using the true edge of the blade for the actions. Work the cuts from various positions of the arms: Shoulder, elbow, and wrist. Focus on casting your actions at the end, and not pulling the cuts. One last note, cuts take space, be very aware of your surroundings during the blocking and performance of the choreography. Give yourself or the performers enough room to effectively carry out the actions and avoid other performers and set pieces.

8

BLOCKS AND PARRIES

Historical vs. Theatrical

One of the biggest differences between historical sword fighting and theatrical sword fighting, aside from the not actually trying to kill each other part, is the way we exaggerate the actions, especially when dealing with how we parry sword attacks in theatrical fighting. When telling a story, we will use larger than needed static blocks to provide a small pause for the audience, allowing them to keep up with the action. Historically, you would never stop moving and every action would have an immediate counter action. When incorporating historical styles to stage, we want to keep that visual energy of historical movement alive while still allowing the audience to keep up with the action. This is where the physical dynamics of a fight come into play for the actors, and why footwork is so important. The swords are only one part of the story, and while we will examine that, we also need to keep in mind how our bodies are telling that story.

Block vs. Parry

For some, the terms **block** and **parry** are completely different and cannot be interchanged. I disagree with that line of thought. However, I do want to take a moment to look at the difference between the two words, especially as they apply to theatrical combat. In his book, Richard Pallaziol states "Blocking refers to stopping the incoming motion of a cut, while parrying is a deflection of a thrust" (Pallaziol, Richard. *The Textbook of Theatrical Combat*. 2006). While Steaphen Fick explains that a block stops the action, and a parry is a redirection of energy (Fick, Steaphen. *The Beginner's Guide to the Long Sword*. Black Belt Communications LLC, 2009). One way I have of explaining this is the term block is for unarmed actions, and a parry is for any weapon actions. However, I have found that the terms block and parry are completely interchangeable, and one should not get too hung up on the terminology.

Edge vs. Flat

The "Edge vs. Flat" debates have been going on for a while now, and it does not look like it's going to stop any time soon. It breaks down to this: Historically, all blocks/parries were made with the flat of the blade not the edge, and on the other side of the argument is that the edge was used in most parries. There is proof with historical antiques in museums proving that both were used. Both sides will keep this debate going for years to come, with solid evidence supporting their claims. But in theatrical combat, our theatrical/prop swords are designed for **edge-to-edge parries**, and we will use a combination of edge and **flat parries** (Figure 8.1), with most of the parries using the edge.

Numbering vs. Names

In most stage combat organizations, the numbering system used in rapier parries is applied to almost all weapons. With rapier being one of the first weapons a student learns, this makes adapting to other weapons much easier. In this chapter, I will be referencing targets of the attack, and describing the various blocks that can be used. I will refer to the stage combat numbering system when it is appropriate with the static blocks.

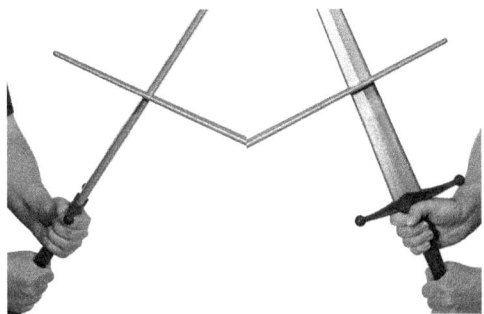

Figure 8.1 Edge v Flat

Static vs. Active Blocks

A **static block** is one that stops the action of the attack through opposition, which is mostly used in theatrical fighting, while an **active block** is one that keeps the energy moving by either redirecting or passing the energy through the intended target area which is utilized in historical fighting. Many times, in theatrical combat, we see the overuse of static blocks being used and thus creating a nonenergetic fight. The key is to utilize more active blocks, while using static blocks strategically to tell the story of the fight. This chapter will focus on the principal techniques of static blocks, and in the next chapter, we will examine active blocks and attacks on the blade while combining these into a dynamic fight.

Static Blocks

Beginning with static blocks, there are several elements we need to keep in mind for each block. The first being proper body alignment during the action. You want your body to create a wall for the incoming attack. This means you will pivot your body toward the block. This also serves the purpose of removing the target from the line of attack.

Next, as stated in the previous chapter, all attacks that are blocked should be cast past the performer and not directing any energy into them, and therefore it is up to the defender to contact the incoming attack.

When performing static blocks on the sword, the defender will be using the **forte** (strong) of the blade to connect with the **foible** (weak) of their partner's blade. There will be exceptions to this in advanced work, but for now, this will be a general rule.

Lastly, keep your elbows slightly bent, do not lock your arms. Even though the energy should be cast, you should not be attacking the incoming attack with stiff arms and heavy energy. Relax, and let the sword do the work for you. Give just enough energy and pressure to stop your partner's blade about 1–2 inches away from their intended target of casting.

Static Blocks on the High Lines

When looking at blocks on the high line, we can break them into defending against attacks to the shoulders and head.

Blocking Cuts to the Shoulders

The first static block we explore is the defense against a cut to the right shoulder (Figure 8.3a).

Starting in Middle Guard, with the right foot forward, pass back with your right foot, and moving your sword at the same time, lift the tip up and push it slightly up and to your right.

Make sure the hilt is not too high, and that you are taking the incoming attack on the forte of your sword, and that the block is edge to edge. In theatrical combat this is referred to as **Parry 3**.

The next static block we explore is the defense against a cut to the left shoulder (Figure 8.3b).

Starting in Middle Guard, with the right foot forward, retreating, move your sword at the same time, lift the tip up, and push it slightly up and to your left.

Make sure the hilt is not too high, and that you are taking the incoming attack on the forte of your sword, and that the block is edge to edge. In theatrical combat, this is referred to as **Parry 4**.

These two parries can be done from any position. The important thing to remember is to keep your tip pulled up and turn your body slightly into the block.

BLOCKS AND PARRIES   87

Figure 8.2 Static Blocks

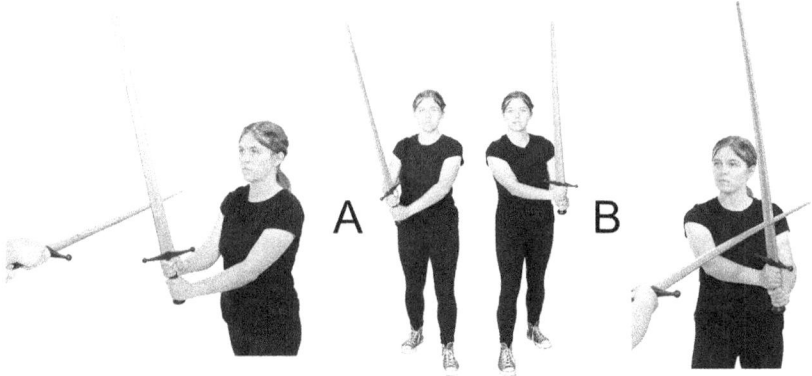

Figure 8.3 Blocks to Shoulders

Blocking attacks to the shoulders with **Hanging Parries**.

A hanging parry is any high line parry where the hilt is above the tip of the sword.

Cuts to the Left Shoulder

Starting in Right Ochs, or a hanging guard on the right with the left foot forward, defend against an attack to the left shoulder by stepping back with the left foot, and moving your sword over to your left, lifting the hilt slightly above your head, and dropping the tip down. Be sure to keep your eyeline clear of obstruction, you should still be able to see your partner, and the audience should be able to see your face.

Starting in Left Ochs, or a hanging guard on the left with the right foot forward, defend against an attack to the left shoulder by retreating, and lifting the hilt slightly above your head, and dropping the tip down.

Cuts to the Right Shoulder

Starting in Left Ochs, or a hanging guard on the left with the right foot forward, defend against an attack to the right shoulder by stepping back with the right foot, and moving your sword over to your right, lifting the hilt slightly above your head, and dropping the tip down. Be sure to keep your eyeline clear of obstruction, you should still be able to see your partner, and the audience should be able to see your face.

Starting in Right Ochs, or a hanging guard on the right with the left foot forward, defend against an attack to the right shoulder by retreating, and lifting the hilt slightly above your head, and dropping the tip down.

Variation

To add a little bit more flair and dynamics to a fight, instead of just moving your sword straight into position, you can add a **Moulinet**. A moulinet, or molinello, is a circular swinging of the sword, like a rolling action.

From the hanging guard position, first roll your tip up and back, then continuing the circle down and around, lift your sword into the hanging block.

Blocking Cuts to the Head

Now, we are going to explore the various static defenses against a cut to the head (Figure 8.3c).

As mentioned in the previous chapter on cuts, vertical, or downward attacks to the head are never aimed at the head or face in theatrical combat; instead, attacks are aimed off target either to the right or left, above the shoulder.

Things to remember when static blocking vertical cuts, always make sure your hilt is opposite the attacked target. If the cut is coming down to your right shoulder, you want to make sure your hilt is on your left side, and vice versa. Unless you're doing a hanging parry or a hero's parry (later in this chapter), keep your sword level, do not allow the sword to be at an angle with either the tip of the sword or the hilt higher than the other end. Doing so will either redirect their attack away from you, or into your hilt.

Vertical Cuts to the Right Shoulder

As your partner initiates their vertical attack to your right shoulder.

From the middle guard position with the left foot forward, pass back with the left foot, and lift your sword up and above your head, with the tip of the sword pointing right, and the hilt above your left shoulder (Figure 8.4a). Make sure your sword is above the top of your head and that you are not obstructing your line of sight. In theatrical combat this is referred to as **Parry 5a**.

From the middle guard position with the right foot forward, retreat and lift your sword up and above your head, with the tip of the sword pointing right, and the hilt above your left shoulder (Figure 8.4a).

Figure 8.4 Blocks to Head Cuts

Vertical Cuts to the Left Shoulder

As your partner initiates their vertical attack to your left shoulder.

From the middle guard position with the left foot forward, retreat and lift your sword up and above your head, with the tip of the sword pointing left, and the hilt above your right shoulder (Figure 8.4b). Make sure your sword is above the top of your head and that you are not obstructing your line of sight. In theatrical combat this is referred to as **Parry 5**.

From the middle guard position with the right foot forward, pass back with the left foot, and lift your sword up and above your head, with the tip of the sword pointing left, and the hilt above your right shoulder (Figure 8.4b).

Static Blocks on the Low Lines

When looking at blocks on the low line, we can break them into defending against attacks to the hips and legs. Although in theatrical combat we only target the hips and not the legs, unless we are doing a swipe, and the defender is avoiding with a jump (see chapter on Advanced Cuts and Kills).

Blocking Cuts to the Hips

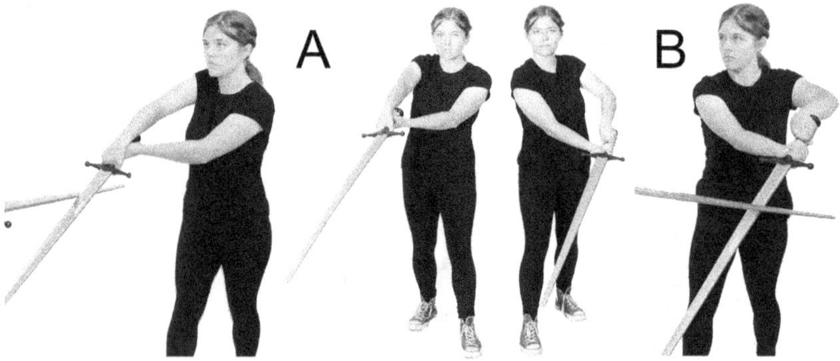

Figure 8.5 Blocks to the Hips

Cuts to the Right Hip

From the middle guard position with the right foot forward, pass back with the right foot, lift your sword hilt, and drop the tip of the sword, using a counterclockwise motion with your hands. Your right hand should be in pronation (Figure 8.5a). In theatrical combat this is referred to as **Parry 2**.

From the middle guard position with the left foot forward, retreat and lift your sword hilt and drop the tip of the sword, using a counterclockwise motion with your hands. Your right hand should be in pronation.

Cuts to the Left Hip

From the middle guard position with the right foot forward, retreat and lift your sword hilt and drop the tip of the sword. Your right hand should be in supination (Figure 8.5b). In theatrical combat this is referred to as **Parry 7**.

From the middle guard position with the left foot forward, pass back with the left foot, lift your sword hilt, and drop the tip of the sword. Your right hand should be in supination (Figure 8.5b).

Blocking Thrusts to the Torso

Thrust can be an exciting action to add in a fight, and the static blocks to the action should be just as exciting, even though the actions themselves are simple.

Starting in Middle Guard, with the right foot forward, pass back with your right foot, and moving your sword at the same time, circle the tip in a clockwise direction and push the thrust aside to your right (Figure 8.6a).

Starting in Middle Guard, with the left foot forward, pass back with your left foot, and moving your sword at the same time, circle the tip in a counterclockwise direction and push the thrust aside to your left (Figure 8.6b).

Make sure the hilt is not too high and that you start the block on your foible or middle of the blade and end with their blade on the forte of your sword.

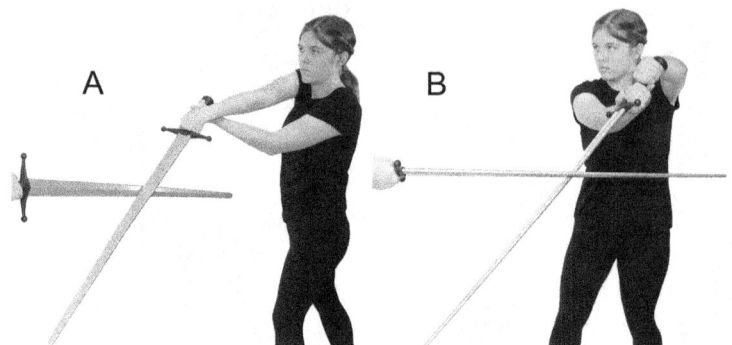

Figure 8.6 Blocks to Thrusts

Specialty Blocks and Actions

The Hero's Parry

The **Hero's Parry** (also known as a sloped parry or waterfall parry) is a variation of the hanging parry from earlier with the addition of a displacement away and creating a sloping of both body and blade (Figure 8.7).

Vertical Attack to the Right Shoulder

From the middle guard with the right foot forward, go into the hanging guard with your hilt on your left side, tip on your right. Displace straight left with your left foot, keeping your right foot in place. Allow your weight to shift to the left, and by lifting your hilt, the angle of the sword will match the angle of your lean (Figure 8.7a).

Vertical Attack to the Left Shoulder

From the middle guard with the right foot forward, go into the hanging guard with your hilt on your right side, tip on your left. Displace straight right with your right foot, keeping your left foot in place. Allow your weight to shift to the right, and by lifting your hilt, the angle of the sword will match the angle of your lean (Figure 8.7b).

BLOCKS AND PARRIES   93

Figure 8.7 Hero's Parry

Figure 8.8 Behind the Back Block

The Behind-the-Back Block

I will admit this is a ridiculous block, nowhere near historically accurate, and is 100% theatrical. However, it can be fun to add into choreographies that need an element of fantasy or humor. If you are choreographing a fight for the play *She Kills Monsters* by Qui Nguyen, or you want Robin Hood to have a little moment, this is a fun little addition to the action.

This move depends on the attacking partner giving a **vocal cue** as this is a **blind parry**. The attack is coming to the upper back of the defender, and they will parry it without looking or turning around.

The attacker starts the attack to the defender's upper back and provides the defender with a vocal cue of some kind. This can be a yell, a loud grunt, or any vocal sound needed for the defender to know the attack is incoming.

The defender, from any guard or position, will roll their sword around their body, hilt above the head, and tip down, until the sword is fully behind the defender, where the attacker will contact it. From here the defender can transport the blade up and over or turn around and continue the fight.

Reinforced Static Parries

Many of the static blocks can be reinforced with a hand on the blade. This can provide additional support for counter attacks, or is used to show how much stronger one character is over another. Here, we will quickly cover **reinforced blocks**, and in a later chapter, we will look at the offensive action called **half swording**.

Reinforced Blocks on the High Line

To reinforce a parry, use the left hand and hold on to the upper part of the blade. The parry is done in the exact same mode as earlier described in this chapter. So you can reinforce the attack to the right shoulder/Parry 3

BLOCKS AND PARRIES 95

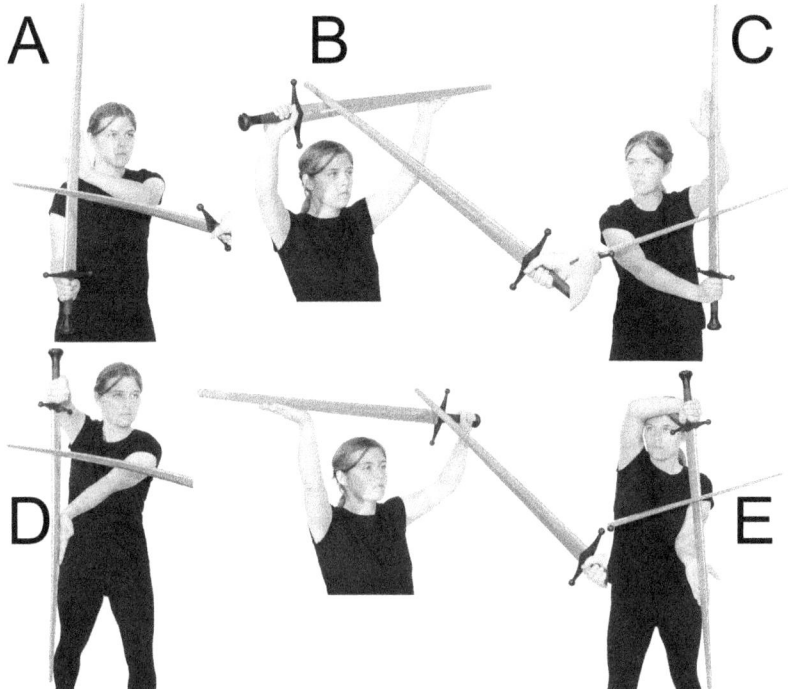

Figure 8.9 Reinforced Parry

(Figure 8.9a), vertical attack to the right shoulder/Parry 5 (Figure 8.9b), and the attack to the left shoulder/Parry 4 (Figure 8.9c).

You can perform these as hanging parries by putting the hilt up and tip down. This can be done for both the attack to the right shoulder (Figure 8.9d) and the attack to the left shoulder (Figure 8.9e). However, one thing you want to be aware of is not letting your fingers of your left hand get in the path of the attacking blade. Notice that with both parries, the left hand is open, and the fingers are removed from the path of the blade.

If you want to reinforce the Parry 5a/vertical attack to the left shoulder, you will need to keep your left hand on the handle, and your right hand will hold the blade (Figure 8.9f).

Drills

Below are sample drills you can do to build proficiency with the various blocks you learned in this chapter.

Nonpartnered Drill 1

From each guard position, move in and out of the blocks, working your way around.

Example: Start in low guard, block an attack to the left hip, and recover back to low guard. Next block an attack to the right hip and then recover back to low guard. Follow this with blocking attacks to the right shoulder, vertical attack down on the right shoulder, vertical attack down to the left shoulder, and finish with blocking an attack to the left shoulder. Making sure to reset back into low guard between each action. Next move to the middle guard and repeat the drill.

Nonpartnered Drill 2

In this drill block, the same attack patterns as before, but instead of resetting to the previous guard, change to a new guard.

Example: Start in low guard, block an attack to the left hip, and recover to middle guard. Next block an attack to the right hip and then recover back to hanging guard. Continue this pattern and mix up the guards used as much as possible.

Partnered Drill 1

In this drill, Partner A will Attack, and Partner B will Block. Both partners start in low guard, A will attack the left hip, B will Block. Both partners will reset back to their guard, then continue the same actions around: Right hip, right shoulder, vertical attack to the right shoulder, vertical attack to the left shoulder, left shoulder, then swap and let A defend while B attacks. You can do this drill from any guard position or mix them up during the drill.

The key to this drill is to make sure that both partners are moving, and keeping the distance between them, and that the attacker is casting their actions and the defender is meeting their blade.

Partnered Drill 2

In this drill, the fighters will not reset between actions, and instead will go from the block to an attack.

Both partners start in middle guard, or it can be any guard you want. Partner A attacks B's left hip. B blocks, then from the block, attacks A's left hip. A Blocks, then returns the attack, this time to B's right hip. This continues back and forth until both partners have attacked and defended all targets.

Partnered Drill 3

This is a fun drill of deception.

This drill is the same as Partnered drill 1, with two exceptions, the first is that the partners are slightly out of distance, and the second one is that the partner performing the blocks decides which blocks to take and which attacks to ignore. This drill ensures that the attacking partner is casting their cuts properly.

Closing Comments

In looking at the theatrical parry numbers you may be asking yourself, where are parries 1 and 6 (and if you're experienced in rapier for stage, you're also asking about 8). Well, those parries are not really used in theatrical fighting with broadsword. Here, we are focusing on creating a box around the performer.

As before with attacks, while defending you want to pay attention to the distance between performers. Too close and it can be both unsafe and poor looking, too far apart and it looks unbelievable.

Finally, pay attention to casting. When blocking, it is easy to send excessive energy into your partner's blade during the attack.

9

ACTIVE BLOCKS AND ATTACKS ON THE BLADE

Historical vs. Theatrical

In this chapter, we are going to be deep diving into many of the elements of historical sword fighting that give it its excitement and dynamics. Here is where the swords stay in constant motion while trying to manipulate and control one another, work toward an opening for an attack, faint, twist, turn, circle, and deceive. Yet we are going to do all this safely. In the original historical text, many attacks are aimed at the head and face, so we will be adjusting those targets of the actions. Remember, in theater, we never aim an attack toward our partners' head or face. While some historical purist may claim this completely takes away from the intent of historical work, I disagree. If our work is still based in historical sources, and the only thing we adjust is for safety, I believe we can achieve historical accuracy in our work.

Avoiding the Face

In all active blocks and manipulations of the blade, it is important to focus on not just controlling the blade, but also the tips of the swords. This is the responsibility of both performers. Never should the tips or swords cross in front of or toward the face. Always make sure that all manipulations go over the head and are completely clear of the face.

Active Blocks

Active blocks are dynamic movements that block an incoming attack by either deflecting or redirecting the energy of the attacker's blade, while at the same time keep the defender's blade in movement in preparation for a **counterattack**. Like static blocks, active blocks require proper body alignment, and while you want your body to create a wall for the incoming attack, you also need to stay mobile and active. This allows you to be ready to move in any direction and counter with a cut appropriate to the open targets.

Later in this chapter, we will look at actions against the blade after a block, so for now, we are going to focus on active blocks that attack the incoming blade or just redirect its energy, either by displacement or by continuing its energy.

One key to remember when deflecting or redirecting an attack is to never redirect it into your own body or toward your face. I know that sounds like an obvious rule, but you would be surprised how easy it is to do if you are not paying attention.

Active Blocks on the High Lines

As before with the static blocks, our areas of attack are the same on all lines. However, unlike static blocks, we are not stopping the action of the incoming blade and need to learn how to control the attack coming into each target zone.

Let's start our journey into active blocks with one of the most common attacks from a right-handed partner, the diagonal attack to the left shoulder. The blocks below will work against cuts to either shoulder. To switch to an attack on the other side, just swap your feet and direction of block and attack.

Attacks to the Shoulders

The first action we are going to take against this cut is a quick **circling/passthrough parry**, with a retreat, then an advance with thrust.

Starting in middle guard with the right foot forward, when the attacker moves forward with the cut to the left shoulder (Figure 9.1a), the defender should quickly retreat while circling the tip of the sword down and in a clockwise motion to connect with the false edge of the incoming attack (Figure 9.1b). Once contact is made, add some pressure to the blade, ensuring it continues past the target out of distance (Figure 9.1c). Once the blade clears the body, extend your sword toward "Center" (here, we will pull the target off-line to the right of our partner's waist) and pass forward with the left foot. The original attacking partner will either need to escape by moving away or immediately parry the attack.

The next active block we are going to take against this cut is a **striking parry**, with a retreat, then a counter cut to the left hip.

Start in either a high guard or high right guard with the left foot forward (Figure 9.2a). As the attack comes forward toward the left shoulder, pass back with the left foot and bring your sword down from high left to low striking the incoming attack (Figure 9.2b). Continue your sword's action until the opposing sword is past your body (Figure 9.2c). Once the sword is clear, roll your sword into a cut to the left hip with an advance. The original attacking partner will either need to escape by moving away, or immediately parry the attack.

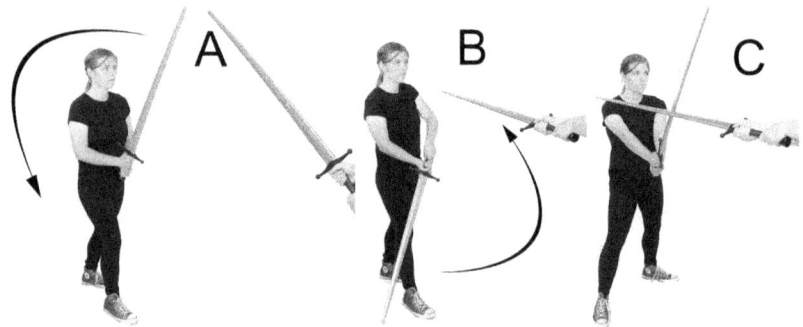

Figure 9.1 Circling Parry

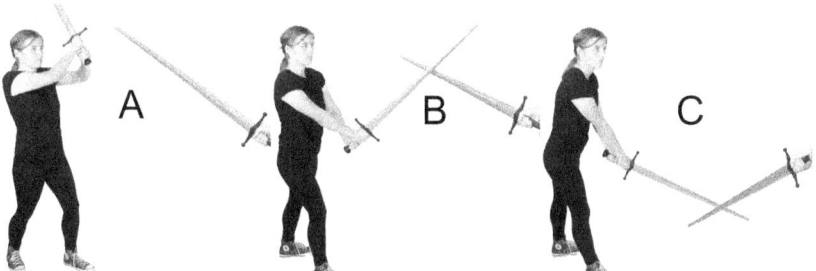

Figure 9.2 Striking Parry

The last active block we are going to take against this cut is a **knock-away parry**, with a retreat, then a counter vertical cut to the right shoulder.

The defender will start in a low guard with the left foot forward (Figure 9.3a). As the attack comes forward, retreat with the left foot and with a curving **Lifting cut** – a cut with the false edge that curves out then back in during the action, strike the back/underside of the incoming attack (Figure 9.3b). Once the contact has been made and the incoming attack is knocked away and off-line (Figure 9.3c), continue your lift and counterattack with a vertical cut down to the right shoulder. The original attacking partner will either need to escape by moving away or immediately parry the attack.

Vertical Attacks to the Head

Now, we will explore the active blocks against downward vertical attacks.

First, we will explore a **deflective parry** with a displacement.

This action may feel familiar, as we are incorporating the hanging parry from the previous chapter with a displacement and counterattack.

Here, both partners start in a high guard, left foot forward. As the attack comes down toward the left shoulder, the defender displaces straight right with the right foot, while circling the sword down and up into a hanging parry with the hilt on the right. The attack will continue to move down but away from the defender after the deflection, at which point the defender will roll their sword along the left side, and strike with a vertical attack to the left shoulder. The original

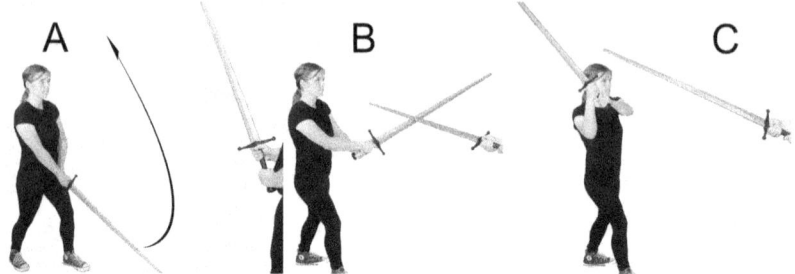

Figure 9.3 Knock-away Parry

attacking partner will either need to escape by moving away or immediately parry the attack.

For a variation of this, once the attack is deflected, pull your sword back into a hanging guard on the right and perform a thrust attack instead of a cut.

Next, we will explore a knock-away parry with a displacement.

Here, both partners start in a high guard, left foot forward. As the attack comes down toward the left shoulder, the defender displaces straight right with the right foot, while knocking the incoming sword aside to the left. The attack will continue to move down but away from the defender after the knock away, the defender will continue the roll of the sword, and strike with an attack to the left shoulder. The original attacking partner will either need to escape by moving away or immediately parry the attack.

Finally, we will explore a **striking parry** with a displacement.

Both partners start in a high guard, left foot forward. As the attack comes down, the defender is going to displace straight right and recover by pivoting toward the attack and passing the left foot back. The defender will strike the back of the opposing sword causing it to continue down. The defender can continue the cut down to the left and roll it into a horizontal or vertical cut from the left. The original attacking partner will either need to escape by moving away or immediately parry the attack.

Active Blocks on the Low Line

First, we will explore a striking parry with counterattack.

Both partners will start in middle guard, left foot forward. As the attacker steps forward and attacks with a cut to the left hip, the defender will cross back with the left foot while rolling the sword down left. Once the defending blade strikes the attack and nullifies its force, continue rolling the blade back and around. Continue with either a horizontal or vertical cut to the right shoulder as you pass forward with the left foot. The original attacking partner will either need to escape by moving away or immediately parry the attack.

Next, we will explore a passthrough parry with counterattack.

Both partners will start in middle guard, left foot forward. As the attacker steps forward and attacks with a cut to the left hip, the defender will cross back with the left foot while rolling the sword over and left coming in behind the attacking blade. Once the defending blade makes contact, continue pushing the blade through. The defender can disengage from the parry and roll the blade into an attack with either a horizontal or vertical cut to the right shoulder as you pass forward with the left foot. The original attacking partner will either need to escape by moving away or immediately parry the attack.

Finally, we will explore a parry that will manipulate the opponent's blade to make way for a counterattack.

Both partners will start in middle guard, left foot forward. As the attacker steps forward and attacks with a cut to the left hip, the defender will cross forward with the left foot and immediately pass back with the left foot and pivot toward the attack; this happens while the defender is going to a low left hip block/perry 7 to stop the attack. Once the defending blade makes contact, and the attack's energy is gone, continue pushing your sword forward, and controlling the blade (more on this below), continue pushing the blade up and over your head. The defender can disengage from the parry and roll the blade into an attack with either a horizontal or vertical cut to the right shoulder as you displace forward left with the left foot. The original attacking partner will either need to escape by moving away or immediately parry the attack.

This is not an easy action to accomplish, and the partners should take their time learning this action in slow motion with zero force behind the cuts. Make sure you are not lifting your partner's blade into your face, but instead are using your sword to guide it up and over, your face/head should always be protected.

Manipulations of the Blade

Binding

In German historical text the term **Binden**, meaning to bind, refers to two weapons making and maintaining contact. The binding of the blades allows for several actions to be performed against the sword and to gain the advantage. In theatrical combat, a bind is a form of **pris d'fer**, a controlling attack on the blade, that carries the opponent's weapon from a high line to a low line on the opposite side, diagonally. We will be exploring more actions on the blade below.

Engaged/Disengaged

Two terms that will be used frequently are **Engaged** and **Disengaged**. These terms refer to the contact made between two swords. If both blades are maintaining contact, that is referred to as engaged. If a sword breaks contact, or is not making contact, it is referred to as disengaged.

Winding

Another term used in German historical manuscripts is Winden. Winden, or **winding**, is an action where the sword winds or turns along the opponent's weapon during a bind. It is used to gain leverage and change the angle of attack to find open targets without losing an advantage. The main issue with using these in stage combat is that they involve the point with a majority of the targets being the face or head. While this can be safely done in film with a qualified fight director, these are a bit too advanced for an introduction book. However, using a different technique explored below, we can approximate them safely for stage, even at the beginner's level.

Pressure Attacks

Pressure attacks utilize a continuous pressure against the opponent's blade in order to control, manipulate, or open up targets. There are basically two types of pressure attacks we use in theatrical combat the **Press** and the **Pressure Glide**.

The Press

The base work of pressure attacks is the Press. The press is basically the art of making contact and pressing the opposing blade away in order to open a target. This can be done from all static blocks on all lines. We will examine a couple of these actions below. The press is not an expulsion. We will look at expulsions further below, but for now understand that a press is an attack on the blade, while an expulsion is something that happens after a flowing attack.

First, we will explore an upward press from a static block.

Both partners start in a middle guard, left foot forward. The attacker cuts to the left shoulder of the defender and the defender is going to block with a static parry to the left shoulder, parry 4, passing the left foot back (Figure 9.4a). Once contact is made, the defender will press against the opposing sword using a quick pushing motion with the arms in an upward diagonal (Figure 9.4b), causing the attacking blade to move up and to the left of the defender. The defender will continue their energy of the press turning it into a cut to the left hip.

Now, we will explore a downward press from a static block.

Both partners start in a middle guard, left foot forward. The attacker cuts to the left shoulder of the defender and the defender is going to block with a static parry to the left shoulder, parry 4, passing the left foot

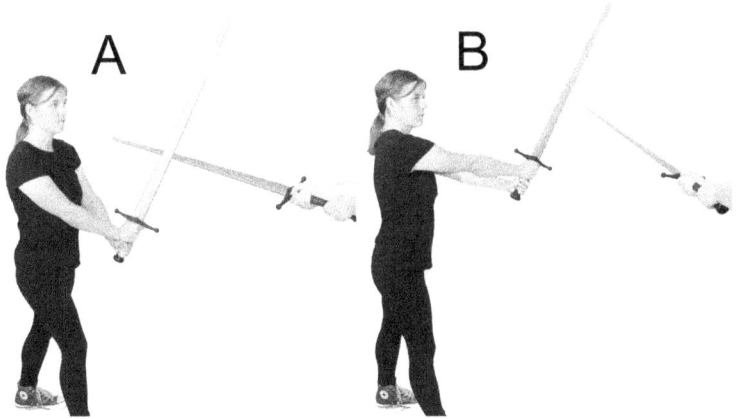

Figure 9.4 Press

back. Once contact is made, the defender will press against the opposing sword using a quick pushing motion with the arms in a downward diagonal, causing the attacking blade to move down to the left of the defender. The defender will continue their energy of the press turning it into a cut to the left shoulder.

The Pressure Glide

Pressure glides, also known as **Froissements,** are strong pressing attacks on the blade that turn into an attack, either a thrust or cut. This requires your partner to maintain pressure against the blade during the action. The blade doing the glide will move from the foible to the forte during the press. Here, pressure glides will only move the opposing weapon to the side, and not in any diagonal or disengaging manner. Know that you can also use a pressure glide to disarm your partner that will be explored more in the next chapter. We will explore both the cut and a thrust from a pressure glide from a static block to the right shoulder, parry 3, but know it can be done from most of the static block positions.

Thrusting to the right shoulder with a pressure glide.

Both partners start in a middle guard, right foot forward. The attacker cuts to the right shoulder of the defender and the defender is going to block with a static parry to the right shoulder, parry 3, passing the right foot back. Once contact is made, the defender will press against the opposing sword out to their right, moving down the blade (Figure 9.5), the defender will drop their tip down towards the attacker's right shoulder and execute a thrust to the target with an advance.

Cutting to the right shoulder with a pressure glide.

Both partners start in a middle guard, right foot forward. The attacker cuts to the right shoulder of the defender and the defender is going to block with a static parry to the right shoulder, parry 3, passing the right foot back. Once contact is made, the defender will press against the opposing sword out to their right, moving down the blade, the defender will roll their tip back, and execute a cut to the attacker's right shoulder.

Figure 9.5 Pressure Glide

Flowing Attacks

Flowing attacks, unlike the previous pressure attacks, don't attack the blade so much as slide along it without excessive force. The main flowing attack is the **glissade**, a gliding action down the blade to a point attack or thrust. Glissades are close to the winding mentioned above; however, they target the four safe areas of your partner – shoulders and hips, and only use thrusting actions. Below we will examine a glissade from a parry 3, cut to the right shoulder, and respond with a thrust to the left shoulder.

The Glissade

Both partners start in a middle guard, right foot forward. The attacker cuts to the right shoulder of the defender and the defender is going to block with a static parry to the right shoulder, parry 3, passing the right foot back (Figure 9.6a). Once contact is made, the defender will maintain

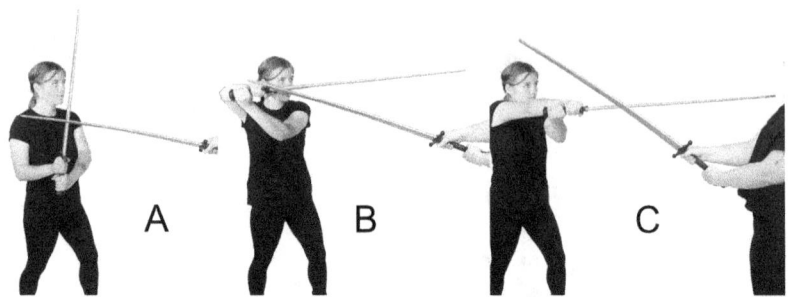

Figure 9.6 Glassade

contact with the opposing sword while lifting the hilt and dropping the tip toward their partner's right shoulder (Figure 9.6b), the defender executes a thrust to the target with an advance while maintaining contact with the opposing blade (Figure 9.6c).

Yielding Parries

A great way to respond to either a pressure glide or a glissade is to use a yielding or ceding parry. A yielding parry is one that moves with the action, not breaking contact, and in the final action of the attack shifts the pressure on the blades. For this example, we are going to look at the last stages of the previous action, the glissade thrust to the right shoulder.

After the initial contact is made after the attack, the defender will maintain contact with the opposing sword while lifting the hilt and dropping the tip toward their partner's right shoulder, the defender executes a thrust to the target with an advance while maintaining contact with the opposing blade (Figure 9.7b). The original attacker will maintain the contact on the incoming blade and shift into a parry 3 with a retreat (Figure 9.7c).

Pris d'fer

Another great element of theatrical sword play that is constantly employed in choreographies is the pris d'fer. A pris d'fer is a taking of the blade attack that once the blade is parried, it is then controlled with either a **croisé**, **bind**, or an **envelopment**. Like the pressure attacks

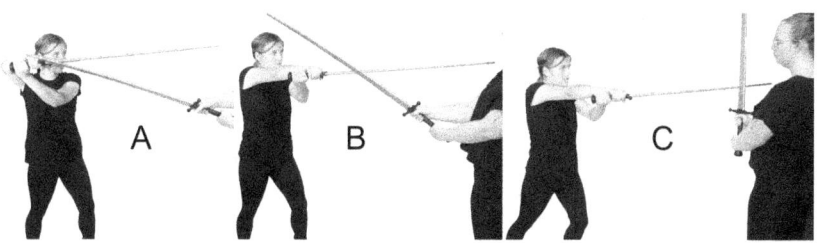

Figure 9.7 Yielding Parry

from earlier, these actions require both performers to apply pressure to the blade; however, the one being controlled needs to allow their blade to move with their partner's action. If the original attacker is placing too much pressure on the blades, the defender will not easily be able to manipulate the swords, and the flow of the moment will be lost. Both should give just enough pressure to maintain contact and allow the control to happen. The focus of energy is from the wrist; however, with the larger envelopment, the full arms can be used to show greater force. When a parry also includes a pris d'fer, it is referred to as a **transport Parry**.

All these actions can be finished with an **expulsion**. Though this technique is more apt for rapier play, it can be added here in broadsword and can add an exciting element to a fight to help create more dynamics. We will explore each one below.

Croisé

The croisé is one of the attacks on the blade associated with pris d'fer. It moves the attacking weapon from a high to a low line, or low to high, on the same side of the body (Figure 9.8a).

Bind

The bind is the second of the attacks on the blade associated with pris d'fer, and as stated earlier in the chapter, carries the opponent's weapon from a high to a low line, or low to high, on the opposite side, diagonally (Figure 9.8b).

110 ACTIVE BLOCKS AND ATTACKS ON THE BLADE

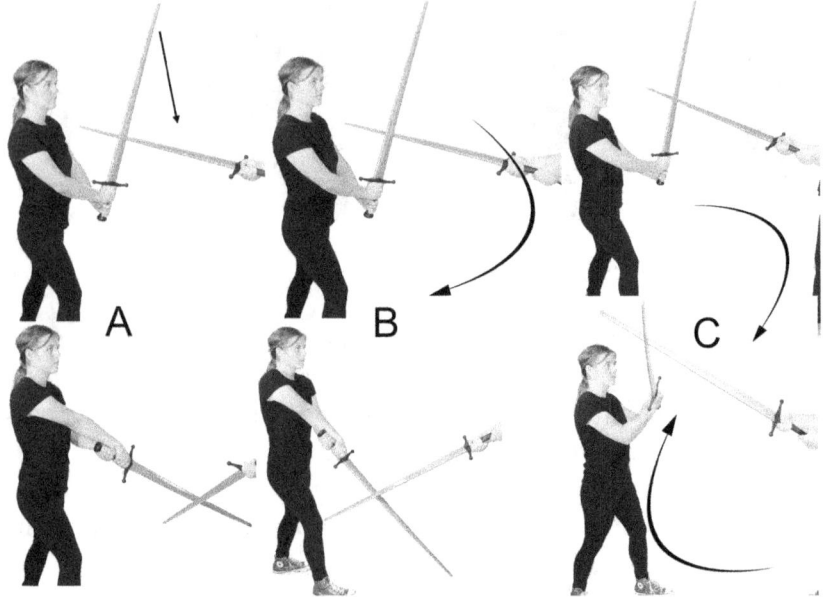

Figure 9.8 Pris d'fer

Both the croisé and bind are great actions to use if you want to take the opponent's blade down to the ground. This will be explored more in the next chapter.

Envelopment

The envelopment is the last of the attacks on the blade associated with pris d'fer and carries the opponent's weapon around in a full circle, starting and ending in the same position (Figure 9.8c).

Expulsions

Expulsions are a great finishing action to any pris d'fer, as it sends the blade away from the body with a bit of force from the action. This action is executed by adding a small flick to the tip of the sword at the end of the action, causing the opponent's blade to leave the engagement. Be aware, that this could actually disarm your partner if they do not have a solid grip on their sword.

Drills

Below are some sample drills you can do to build proficiency with the various actions you learned in this chapter. In these drills, Partner A will initiate the Attack, and Partner B will Block.

Active Parry Drill 1

Drill focus: Passthrough Parries

Both partners start in middle guard, A will attack the left hip, B will circle up and over, and coming from behind the attack pass it through while retreating. Both partners will reset back to their guard, then continue the same actions around: Right hip, right shoulder, left shoulder, then swap and let A defend while B attacks. You can do this drill from any guard position or mix them up during the drill.

Active Parry Drill 2

Drill focus: Striking parries

Both partners start in middle guard, A will attack the left hip, B will strike the attack with a parry 7, then return a cut to A's left hip. Both partners will reset back to their guard, then continue the same actions around: Right hip, right shoulder, left shoulder, then swap and let A defend while B attacks. Counter attacks should mirror the initial attack. You can do this drill from any guard position or mix them up during the drill.

Active Parry Drill 3

Drill focus: Knock-away parries

This drill will use only cuts to the shoulders, both horizontal and vertical.

Partner A starts in High Guard, partner B starts in Low Guard. A attacks with a cut to the left shoulder; B lifts their blade, knocking away the attack as they retreat, and responds with a cut to the left shoulder with an advance. Reset between each attack, then swap and let A defend while B attacks. Counter attacks should mirror the initial attack.

Pressure Attacks Drill 1

Drill focus: Presses

Both partners start in middle guard, A will attack to the left hip, B will parry 7, press the attack out, and then return a cut to A's left hip. Both partners will reset back to their guard, then continue the same actions around: Right hip, right shoulder, left shoulder, then swap and let A defend while B attacks. Counter attacks should mirror the initial attack. You can do this drill from any guard position or mix them up during the drill.

Pressure Attacks Drill 2

Drill focus: Pressure Glides

Both partners start in a middle guard. The A cuts to the right shoulder of B who parries with parry 3, passing the right foot back. B will press against the opposing sword out to their right, moving down the blade, then B will drop their tip down toward A's right shoulder and execute a thrust with an advance. Reset between each attack, then continue the same actions around: Right hip, right shoulder, left shoulder. You then swap and let A defend while B attacks.

Pressure Attacks Drill 3

Drill focus: Pris d'fer

In this drill, partners can start in any guard position. A will attack to the left hip, and B will parry then perform a croisé. B can add an expulsion if they want. This will happen with cuts continuing around to the left shoulder, right shoulder, and left hip. On the next rotation, B will execute a bind, then do an envelopment on each of the attacks.

Closing Comments

As stated at the beginning of this chapter, it is very important when dealing with active parries and blade manipulations that performers and directors maintain safety at all times and that the face is never in the path of the weapons. As already stated previously but always worth repeating, pay attention to the distance between performers. Too close and it can be both unsafe and poor looking, too far apart and it looks unbelievable.

Although active parries create a great physicality and dynamics in a fight, you don't want to only use active parries, just as you don't want to only use static parries. Mix up the use of static, active, and blade manipulations to find a good flow and energy to your choreography.

Although we are using some terminology from rapier work, make sure the actions don't start looking like a rapier choreography. Although Errol Flynn could get away with it as Robin Hood, we want to avoid the Hollywood swashbuckling styles with broadsword and ground the fight in more accurate historical use.

If you would like to see some great use of these techniques all can be found in the HBO series Game of Thrones, but I would like to focus on one episode Season 3 episode 2 and look at the bridge fight between Jamie Lannister (Nikolaj Coster-Waldau) and Brienne of Tarth (Gwendoline Christie). During their fight, they do an excellent job of utilizing pressure attacks and yielding parries. C.C. Smiff was swordmaster/fight choreographer; Paul Herbert was the stunt coordinator for that episode. You can find the fight on YouTube.

On a final note – hold on to the sword. With active parries, pressure attacks, and expulsions, it is very easy to lose grip of a sword or have one pushed out of your hand by an over-excited partner.

10

ADVANCED CUTS AND ACTIONS

Safety

Like all fight directors, I know I sound like a broken record when it comes to safety, but I would like to take another moment before starting this chapter to touch base on some topics.

First and foremost, please make sure your equipment is in good working and performance order. Especially for some of these techniques, where there may be contact between the blade and either the performer or their costume. Double check before each rehearsal and performance for any equipment issues, especially burrs or problems with the sword. Some blades have pommels that screw on, and can easily become lose after too much use.

As with any actions in stage combat, we always want to learn the techniques nice and slow and build muscle memory, before even considering moving them to rehearsal speed (usually about ½ or ¾ performance speed). This is especially true when we start dealing with closing actions or killing actions. I know time is always tight in rehearsal, but take the time needed to properly learn the techniques to prevent any form of injuries.

ADVANCED CUTS AND ACTIONS

Make sure both performers are paying attention to each other. Not only is eye contact an important rule in fighting, but even more so when the person is closing in on you with a weapon.

A final note: Make sure both performers are casting their actions and not sending energy into the other performer during an action. If you or another performer need help, review Chapter 7 and refresh on casting.

Swipes

Big sweeping actions of the sword, which appear narrowly avoided by the performer, are always an exciting bit to add into a choreography. These sweeping actions are referred to as **Swipes**, and will target either the legs, belly, or head (Figure 10.1). Now, as with all theatrical actions we never target the head. There are three elements we use to keep performers safe during these actions. The first is we telegraph, followed by keeping the action in check until the performer moves, and we perform out of distance. The attacker should not be swinging their sword like a baseball bat during this action. This needs just as much control, if not more, than any other cut performed toward a performer.

Base Actions of a Swipe

First, the performers are starting off out of distance. The attacker will over prep the action of the swipe. This serves two purposes: First, it

Figure 10.1 Swipes

116 ADVANCED CUTS AND ACTIONS

telegraphs to the other performer the target zone the attacker is swiping and gives the performer a starting place to set; next, the attacker will lead the attack with the pommel of the sword pointing at the target zone and the blade pointing backward, once the performer "clears the area", it can be by leaping/jumping straight up in the air, jumping back pushing with the toes and throwing the butt back, or by squatting (Figure 10.1), the attacker can finish their action with the follow through.

The defender needs to maintain their sword and be aware of the point. For the two jumps, the defender can use their left hand to grab the blade and keep the sword above their head. For the squat, the defender can just tuck their sword into their body (Figure 10.1).

Leg Swipe

As mentioned earlier, the name of the action is misleading, as the performers are not truly targeting the legs. The attacker will over prep the action of the swipe by lifting the sword high and to the right (if doing a right-to-left swipe). This telegraphs the target zone of the legs (Figure 10.2a), next the swing begins, leading with the pommel of the sword pointing at the target zone and the blade pointing backward (Figure 10.2b), once the performer "clears the area", in this action it is by leaping/jumping straight up in the air while lifting the knees (Figure 10.2c), the attacker can finish their action with the follow through and extension

Figure 10.2 Leg Swipe

ADVANCED CUTS AND ACTIONS 117

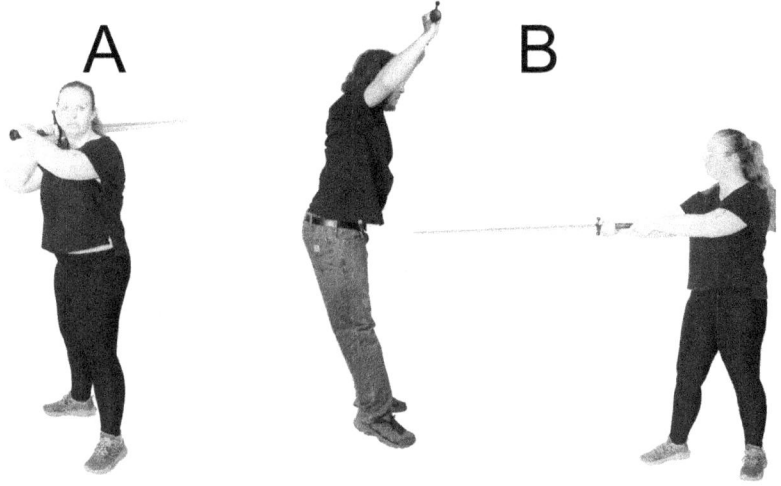

Figure 10.3 Belly Swipe

of the sword (10.2d). The sword is kept "tucked in" and is not extended until the other performer jumps (Figure 10.2c).

Belly Swipe

The attacker will over prep the action of the swipe by bringing the sword to the right (if doing a right-to-left swipe). This telegraphs the target zone of the belly, next the swing begins, leading with the pommel of the sword pointing at the target zone and the blade pointing backward (Figure 10.3a), once the performer "clears the area", in this action it is by jumping up and back, pushing with the toes and throwing the butt back (Figure 10.3b), the attacker can finish their action with the follow through and extension of the sword. The sword is kept "tucked in" and is not extended until the other performer jumps (Figure 10.3b).

Head Swipe

As mentioned earlier, the name of the action is misleading, as the performers are not truly targeting the head, but above where the head would be if the performer doesn't squat. The attacker will over prep the action of the swipe by bringing the sword down to the right (if doing

118   ADVANCED CUTS AND ACTIONS

Figure 10.4 Head Swipe

a right-to-left swipe). This telegraphs the target zone of the head, next the swing begins, leading with the pommel of the sword pointing at the target zone and the blade pointing backward, once the performer "clears the area", in this action it is by squatting down and maintaining eye contact (Figure 10.4b), the attacker can finish their action with the follow through and extension of the sword (Figure 10.4c). The sword is kept "tucked in" and is not extended until the other performer squats. A point to be mindful of is the squat. This is a squat and not a bend. Make sure the performer is squatting down, using their knees, and not just bending forward at the waist.

False Attacks

False Attacks and **Feints** (Fehler in German manuscripts) are actions made with either the sword or the body and are meant to deceive the receiver by misdirecting the action. Such as cuts started to one target area but are either removed, changed, or stopped. These moves are intended to draw out the opponent and create an opening for a different attack.

Stop Short

One of the easiest ways to deliver a false attack is to prep for a cut, begin the first action, then immediately go back into a different guard. For example, starting in middle guard, the performer preps for a cut to the left shoulder, then as the cut just starts, switches to a high guard.

The "attacker" does not do any footwork. To sell this on stage, the defender should throw the parry at the last moment with footwork.

Cuts to Thrusts/Thrusts to Cuts

Cuts to thrusts and thrusts to cuts are fun easy ways to add more dynamics to a fight. Make sure to be aware of spacing, speed, and targeting in this technique. The performers know what's happening, it needs to be a surprise to the audience.

Cut to Thrust

Both performers start in middle guard, left foot forward. The attacker initiates a cut the left shoulder with footwork, as the defender retreats and performs the parry 4, the attacker pulls the blade in before the parry, and with a cross forward left with the left foot, thrusts to the right hip. The defender will need to displace and parry or escape the attack.

Thrust to Cut

Both performers start in middle guard, left foot forward. The attacker initiates a thrust the left hip with footwork, as the defender retreats and performs the parry 7, the attacker pulls the blade in before the parry, and with a cross forward left with the left foot (Figure 10.5a), cuts to the right shoulder. The defender will need to displace and parry or escape the attack.

Change Cut

I will admit this is one of my favorite actions to do with broadswords. It's fast, dynamic, and has many applications. It looks great on stage or on film. But it does take practice and proper timing. Make sure all performers practice this slowly and consistently before any increase in speed happens. This action can be done in either one step, or two, depending on how much movement you need.

Both performers start in middle guard, right foot forward. The attacker (A) initiates a cut at the right shoulder with footwork (Figure 10.5a), as

120 ADVANCED CUTS AND ACTIONS

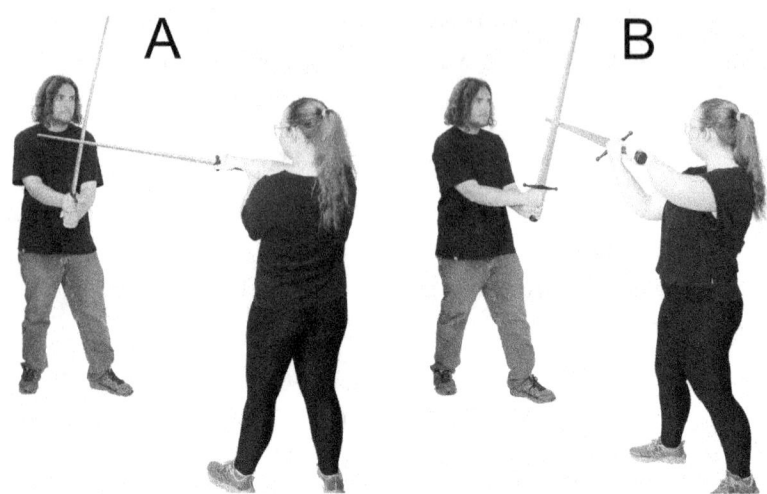

Figure 10.5 Change Cut

the defender (B) retreats and performs the parry 3, A then rolls the cut over to a false-edge attack to the left shoulder (Figure 10.5b). To help A with this cut, they should slip their thumb to the blade while initiating the second action from the wrists. The performers can either just step with the initial action or can step with both cuts.

Performing a false edge cut can be confusing the first time you attempt it. In this action, you will swing the sword to the opposite site without rolling the blade so that the attack is made with the false edge. To perform this smoothly, let your top hand wrist rotate, and the bottom hand do the work of the action.

Half-Swording

Half-swording is a technique where the performer has one hand on the handle and the other on the middle section of their blade (Figure 10.6). Like the reinforced blocks from earlier but chocked down further on the blade. These actions are useful when distance has been closed to where the full use of the sword is impractical. These actions will be explored further in the killing actions section.

Figure 10.6 Half Sword

Closing Actions

Closing actions refer to any action which brings the two performers together in distance close enough to grab ahold of each other. At this distance, full use of the sword is not optional, and the performers will need to change techniques to actions such as half-swording, pummel attacks, disarms, or **grappling** (unarmed combat).

There are various ways performers can close distance in a fight. The easiest method is for only one performer to move during an action. If the Attacker (A) cuts to the Defender's (B) right shoulder with forward footwork, B will not retreat or remove themselves from the attack when they parry. This will close the distance between the combatants.

Another method is for a performer to close distance with a counter action such as a bind or croisé after the block. To perform this, A will attack to B's left shoulder, B will parry 4 with retreat, then as they are binding down, advance in toward A.

If the performers need to be almost body to body or **corps-à-corps**, both can move in at the same time during the attack and block.

Hilt Smashes

A **hilt smash** (also known as a hilt bash or hilt strike) is an attack on the blade done after the block. To perform this action, once A attacks and B successfully blocks, in this situation, A cut to B's left shoulder

ADVANCED CUTS AND ACTIONS

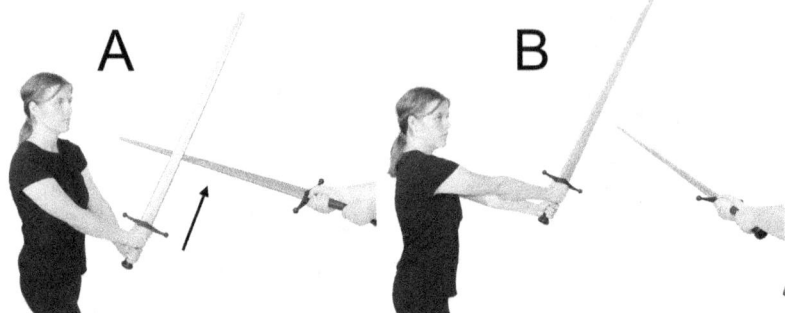

Figure 10.7 Hilt Smash

(Figure 10.7a), B will slightly lower their hilt, maintaining contact with A's sword, B will then quickly bring the cross guard of their hilt into contact with A's sword, directing it up and away (Figure 10.7b). Be careful, too much force and you can send a sword flying out of a performer's hands. This action can be done on all lines of attack. B can retreat with the action, stay in place, or retreat with the cut then advance with the smash.

Pummeling Attacks

Pummeling attacks can take two different forms, the first being an attack with the pommel while one or both hands are on the handle, or while half-swording, and can target almost anywhere you want although most often used for face or stomach attacks. For physical reactions to pain refer to the next chapter.

Basic Pommel Attack to the Face

In this example, the Attacker (A) will keep both hands on the hilt of the sword and attack the "face" of their partner. Starting from a close distance, A will lift their sword up and away from the defender (B) while sliding the left hand down over the pommel. Depending on your staging or camera angle, there are two ways to perform this:

Version A – In profile to the audience (Figure 10.8a)

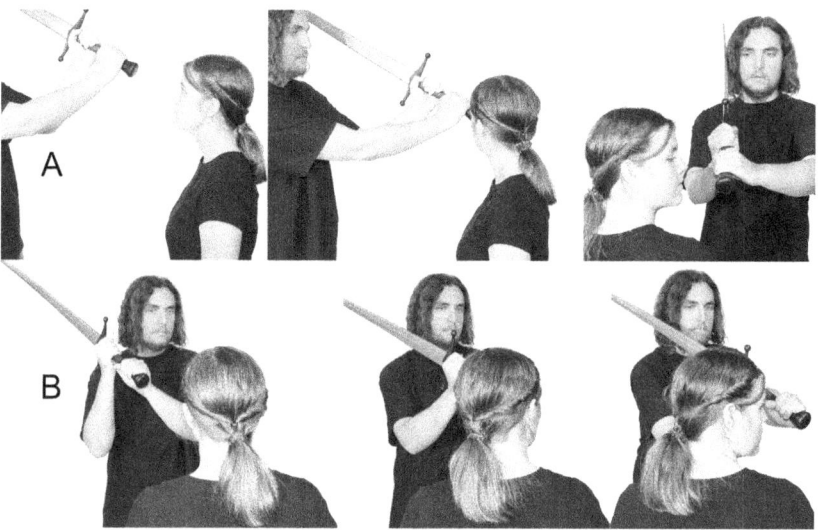

Figure 10.8 Pommel to Face

A will do a quick strike over the upstage shoulder of B and pull back immediately. B will need to perform a **knap** – a slap or hit on the body to create the sound of being hit, along with a vocal and physical reaction to the pain.

Version B – Audience or camera behind a performer (Figure 10.8b)

A will do a quick strike across the face of B and pull back immediately. In this the attack will be a good 8–12 inches away from the actor's face and will do a quick travel from right to left or vice versa. B will need to perform a knap along with a vocal and physical reaction to the pain.

Note: If performing this for film, no knap is needed.

Basic Pommel Attack to the Body

In this example, A will keep both hands on the hilt of the sword and attack the belly of their partner. Starting from a close distance, A will pull their sword away from B while sliding the left hand down over the pommel. Depending on your staging or camera angle, there are two ways to perform this:

Version A – In profile to the audience

124 ADVANCED CUTS AND ACTIONS

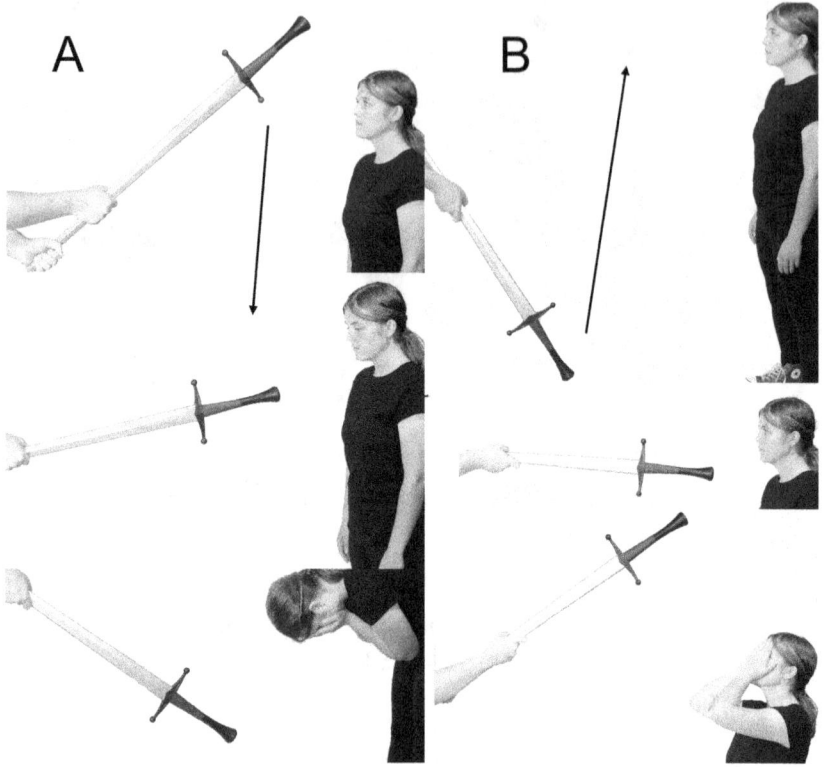

Figure 10.9 Pommel Swing

A will do a quick strike upstage of B's body and pull back immediately. B will need to perform a knap along with a vocal and physical reaction to the pain.

Version B – Audience or camera behind a performer

A will do a quick strike toward the center torso of B and pull back immediately. In this, the attack will be a good 6–8 inches away from the actor's body. B will need to perform a knap along with a vocal and physical reaction to the pain.

Half-Sword Pummeling Attacks

When in half-sword, the attacks work exactly as described above; however, the attacker will be holding the sword by both the handle and the blade.

Swinging Pommel Attack to the Face

I have found keeping one of the actors' back to the audience or camera works best for this action, preferably the one receiving the action. A will keep both hands on the blade of the sword and attack the "face" of their partner. Starting from an extended distance, A will pull their sword away from B; this can either be in an upward (Figure 10.9a) or downward (Figure 10.9b) action. A will perform either a golf swing up or a hammer swing down along the center of B. In this, the attack will be a good 8–12 inches away from the actor's body. B will need to perform a knap along with a vocal and physical reaction to the pain. For a golf swing, the actor reacts back with the head first, and for a hammer, swing reacts down with the head first.

Variation

Performer B can be kneeling during this action.

The Five Master Strikes of Liechtenauer

Finally, we will quickly look at the five cuts Liechtenauer considered the master strikes, or Meisterhau. Some of these you have already learned in the previous chapter. I provide them here as a quick reference and understanding of how these cuts work. They are fun additions to a choreography.

Zornhau "Strike of Wrath" – A high right diagonal attack with pass forward. A simple and easy strike, already learned in Chapter 7.

Krumphau "Crooked Strike" – Diagonal Right to opponents right. This sounds more complicated than it is, and its focus is to strike the hand or right side of the head. Here, we can turn it into a diagonal cut to the shoulder. Starting in a high right guard left foot forward, start the cut without a prepping action and arch the cut from your high right to their right shoulder as you step forward and out with your right foot.

Zwerchhau "Cross Strike" – False edge to their left, true for right. This one can be a bit tricky, as you will be using the false edge of the blade for attacks to your partner's left, and true edge for their right, all while keeping your hilt high. Start in high guard on the right side with the left foot forward, Then lifting your hand as you prep the cut, almost like going into parry 5, roll your cut horizontally to the left shoulder of your partner using the false edge of the blade while stepping out with the right foot.

Schielhau "Squinter" – Hooked strike from high with false edge. Almost identical to the Zwerchhau, this cut twists into the partner's right shoulder in a vertical cut. Start in high guard on the right side with the left foot forward, Then lifting your hand as you prep the cut, almost like going into parry 5, start to roll your cut then hook it over to the right shoulder of your partner using the false edge of the blade while passing forward with the right foot.

Scheitelhau "Parting Strike" – Outreaching the attack. This one is basic, and not something we can use much in stage. Here anytime an attack comes to the low line, one simply reaches out and strikes the head of the opponent while avoiding the low attack, as a high attack can out reach a low attack.

Closing Comments

Should the performers wear gloves? I believe if it makes them comfortable while learning the techniques then yes, but when it comes to the choreography, my main question is "Are the characters wearing gloves?", if so, then yes learn the choreography with gloves, if not, don't.

As always pay attention to distance with these actions. It can be very easy to be too close and cause an accident.

As mentioned earlier, be careful with the energy put into the swords on several of these actions, as it can be very easy to knock a sword out of someone's hands if not controlled.

One could easily create a simple choreography without any of the techniques in this chapter, and it will serve the purpose of telling the story, however, adding some of these elements into a choreography will take it to the next level and give you a more dynamic and energetic fight.

11

KILLING ACTIONS AND ADDING FLAIR

Here, we look at adding those final elements to a choreography, death, and flair. Not all fights need flair, and maybe not all fights need killing actions, but for those that do, we want to make sure they look great. We will also look at disarms, as they can add a nice element to a choreography and allow a bit of heightened tension or dynamics to a fight. We will finish the chapter with a quick look at the physical reactions to pain to help sell the action of the fight.

Killing Actions

Killing actions come in two varieties, cuts and thrusts. The choice of killing may completely depend on either the script or the budget. Can your production afford fake blood? Do you need the audience to see the blood, or can the actor turn upstage or away from the camera? Is it a quick or slow action? Can the kill happen off-stage/camera as in Macbeth's death in Shakespeare's MacBeth? These are the decisions the director will have to make when it comes time to kill. Below are a couple

DOI: 10.4324/9781003327622-11

of easy techniques for killing actions, both cuts and thrusts, that with proper blocking will look great to the audience.

Killing Cuts

Cuts are one of the most common ways to kill or injure with a broadsword. Depending on your staging and budget, we will determine which is best for your choreography. We will start with the easiest of all to perform, the killing cut out of distance, then we will look at some simple cuts in distance. These are a little trickier and require a bit more work and staging, but once mastered can be a great element to add to your production. Especially if you have a large fight scene or have a character who has to dispatch several attackers.

Out of Distance

This is the easiest of all killing actions to do, as the actors are safely apart, and no contact with the blade or costume happens. With the performers staged in an upstage-downstage action, the cut can be either horizontal (Figure 11.1a) or vertical (Figure 11.1b), and the victim can turn with the action either upstage or downstage depending on the staging. The goal here is to see the sword pass through the body of the performer. This is done by exaggerating the action of the cut. For a vertical/diagonal cut, we need to see the blade above the performer, and at the end of the cut, pass past the performer (Figure 11.1a). For the horizontal cut across the torso, the same rules apply, we need to see the sword go through the performer. This starts with an exaggerated wind up to the side, and a full pass through the body (Figure 11.1b). It is important that the performers do not close distance during this action and that the "victim" sales the pain with both vocal and physical reaction (see below).

If the killing cut is coming from behind the victim, then the attacker needs to provide a **vocal cue** to the other performer.

Cuts in Distance

Killing cuts in distance happen in two varieties, contact and noncontact. The biggest safety rules here are to always make sure blades are in good

KILLING ACTIONS AND ADDING FLAIR

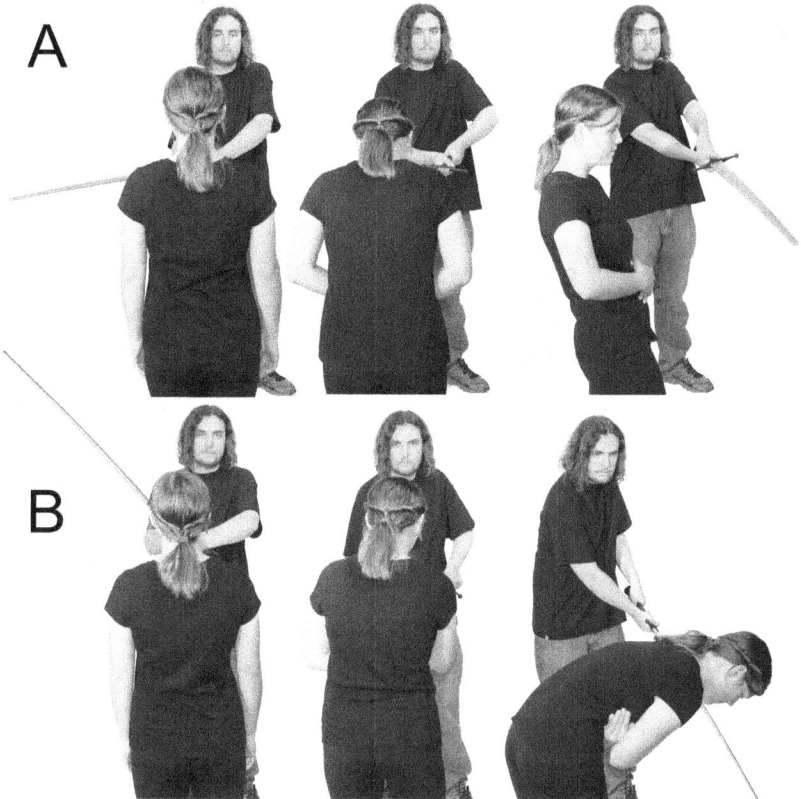

Figure 11.1 Cuts out of Distance

condition, these actions should not be rushed, always keep the flat of the blade toward your partner in these actions, never the edge of the sword, and never place the blade on skin, always on the costume.

Noncontact Killing Cuts

These are performed in distance, but do not make contact with the victim. This action can be performed from any side. For a horizontal cut across the belly/torso, the Attacker (A) preps the attack by pulling the sword flat in to their body, while stepping in and closing distance to the

130 KILLING ACTIONS AND ADDING FLAIR

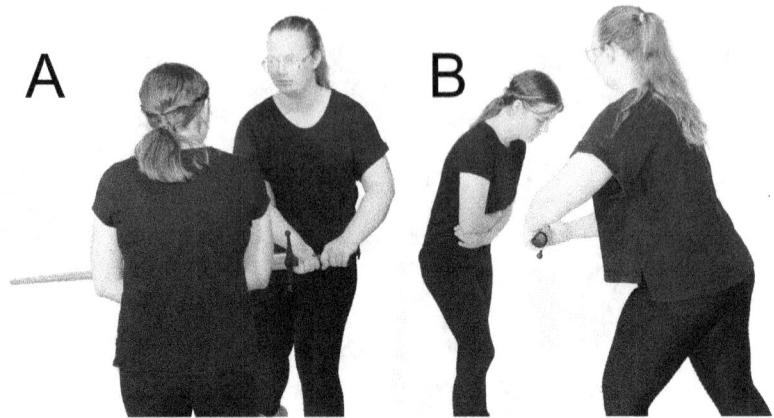

Figure 11.2 Noncontact Cut

Victim (B) (Figure 11.2a) and keeping the sword close to their body (Figure 11.2b), B reacting, then A stepping out and extending the sword out and away from B.

This action can be performed on an upward diagonal as well as the horizontal, the actions are the same as above, with the two exceptions being A preps the attack at an angle with the tip down about 45 degrees, and the elbow up, and on the step out, extend the sword up and away.

Contact Killing Cuts

Taking the above action with a slight modification will be our introduction to contact cuts. These are performed in distance and make contact the victim's torso. For a horizontal cut across the belly/torso, the Attacker (A) preps the attack by pulling the sword in flat, after stepping in and closing distance to the Victim (B), A will place the flat of the blade on B's stomach (Figure 11.3a) and keeping light contact with the sword B reacts to the placement (Figure 11.3b), then A, pulls the sword through without pressing into B, stepping out and extending the sword out and away from B.

Be aware of your blade, and do not twist the sword through the action, as that may cause the edge of the sword to push into your partner.

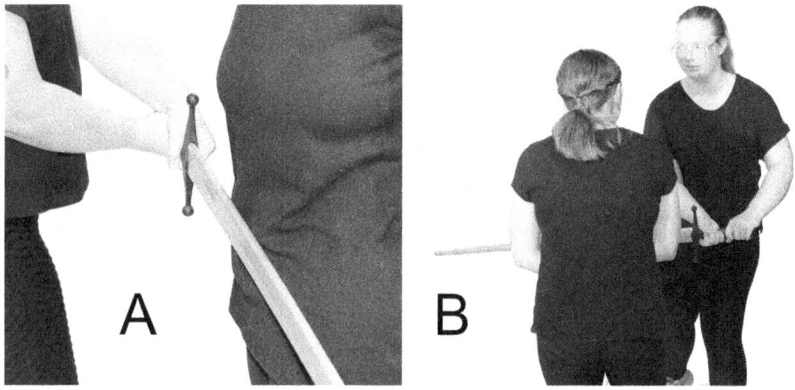

Figure 11.3 Contact Cut

Half-Sword Killing Cut

When the killing cut needs to be up-close and personal, a half-sword cut to the throat makes that happen. This action is accomplished by pulling the blade away from the performer and not across them.

A starts the action in half-sword, with the left hand holding the blade, right hand on the handle. A steps in and places the foible of the blade on B's right shoulder. To execute this cut, A pulls the blade in toward themselves, then across the body keeping several inches away from the throat. B reacts with the action. This can be covered by either the attacker or victim's body covering the line of sight to the audience.

Killing Thrusts

The next killing action we will briefly explore is death by thrust. This action is easy to perform but requires both partners working together to sell the action. Although the attacker controls the targeting of the action, the victim is in full control.

Thrust to the Torso

This action is performed in profile with the Attacker stage left and the victim stage right. The thrust should happen upstage of the audience or

132 KILLING ACTIONS AND ADDING FLAIR

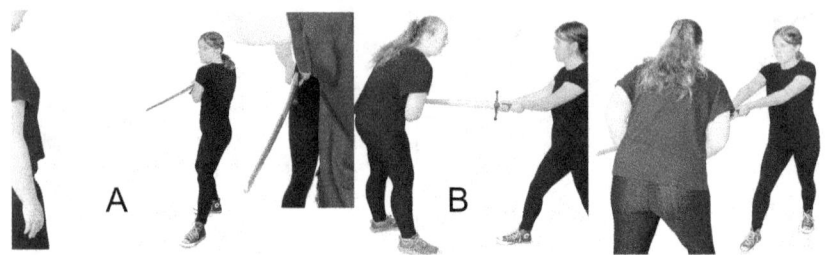

Figure 11.4 Thrust to Torso

camera. The Attacker (A) will perform a thrust to the Victim's (B) left flank with a straight thrust in distance. A prepares the action of the thrust by pulling back and aiming off-line to B's left side (Figure 11.4a). As A thrusts, B turns into the action (Figure 11.4b), and B can choose to cover the action with their hand if they want, as A pulls the thrust back B should twist with the action. If you are going to use the hand to cover the action, make sure to keep the hand clear until the move has been executed, then cover the blade with the hand.

This action can also be performed from the half-sword position.

Note: Be careful not to extend the thrust too far forward, as it will give the illusion of the thrust going all the way through the victim, and they will look more like a kabab than a death.

Variation

If you want to add another element to this kill, instead of pulling the sword out, the attacker can kick the victim off the sword.

After the killing thrust has landed (Figure 11.5a), A can lift their leg, and place their foot safely on B's hip (Figure 11.5b), then B will sell the push back as A's foot follows the action (Figure 11.5c). A must not apply any pressure to this kick and should only be following B's reaction, as the victim is always in control of the action.

Disarms

Sometimes you just need to remove a weapon from someone or from the fight, and the best way to do that is to disarm them. Disarms can be

KILLING ACTIONS AND ADDING FLAIR   133

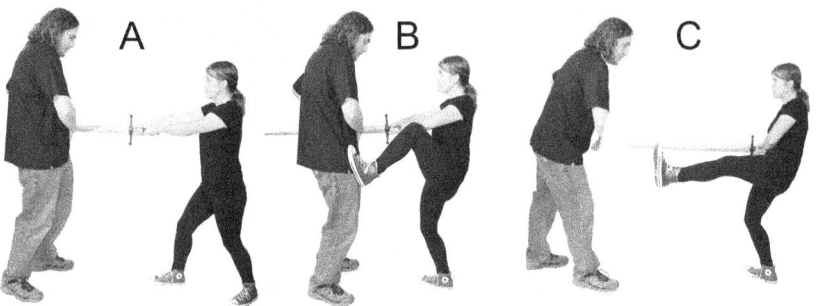

Figure 11.5 Kick Off

classified into two types, drops and takes. Either the performer will have to drop the sword, or the other performer takes their sword away from them. We will explore both types, but first we need to look at controlling the sword when dropped.

Dropping the Sword

Believe it or not, dropping the sword is not as easy as it sounds, and if not done properly, it can cause a lot of problems in theatre. We want to drop the sword in a way that will not cause damage to the weapon, damage to the set, or become a safety or tripping hazard later. And most of all, we want to control where that weapon goes at all times, and never send it into the pit or the audience.

Even though it will appear that the aggressor (A) is knocking the sword out of the victim's (B) hands, B must be in full control of the drop every time.

The first method is the tip-down drop.

Here, the victim already has the tip on the ground and just releases the handle of the sword. It is best practice to keep the sword offline with the body. Making sure the cross hilt is level with the ground, once the sword is in place B lets go of the sword without adding any extra momentum to the handle. If B adds momentum to the handle, the tip could bounce back up.

The next method is the flat drop.

Here, the victim holds the sword level with the ground, then B lets go of the sword without adding any extra momentum. As before, if B adds momentum or spinning, the tip could bounce back up, or the sword could go bouncing across stage.

Bouncing and sliding are bigger issues on stages if you are in dirt or grass the chances of bouncing and slides are greatly reduced, but never zero.

Disarm from the Pris D'fer

A great way to disarm a character is by performing a pris d'fer where the sword ends up touching the ground and the attacker kicking the sword down. With these disarms, you can use a croisé or bind to disarm on the ground.

From the Croisé – A blocks a cut to the left shoulder, then performs a croisé down, pushing the sword tip onto the ground (Figure 11.6a), then stepping into the action will "stomp" on the blade (Figure 11.6b), causing B to do a tip-down drop (Figure 11.6c). Again, B should be in full control of the action, and A does not put any energy into the stomp.

Variation

Instead of the attacker stomping the sword, they can do a hilt smash to the blade causing it to go to the ground. Be careful with this, as B should still be controlling the energy of the drop and not let the smash send the blade flying across the stage.

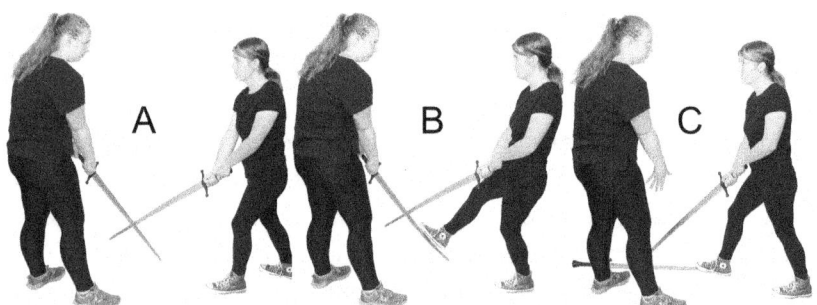

Figure 11.6 Stomp Disarm

Taking the Sword

The safest way to disarm someone is just to take the sword out of their grip. Here, we are going to explore a few simple taking of the sword from engagements.

The first one is just the simple grabbing of the handle.

From a bind, A will reach over and grab the handle of B's sword and twist it from their grip. This starts in a bind in close distance (Figure 11.7a), A will reach over and place their hand either on the pommel or in-between B's hands if the handle is long enough (Figure 11.7b), A then lifts the hilt of their sword, sliding it along the blade toward the hilt of the opposing blade, and pulls with their left hand at the same time (Figure 11.7c), B releases the sword into A's grip. A is not using force to remove the sword, and B is selling the force and controlling the release to A.

This can be done on any line, and either hand can do the grab depending on the best angle of removal.

The next disarm is going to be a leverage technique where A will pull the sword away from B.

Leveraging the Sword Down

This starts in a high left bind (Figure 11.8a), A will reach over and grab the middle of B's blade (Figure 11.8b), A then lifts the hilt of their sword up and over the hilt of B's sword (Figure 11.8c), A pulls their hilt down toward them, pulling B's sword from their hand (Figure 11.8d). Be careful not to trap B's hand or fingers between the swords.

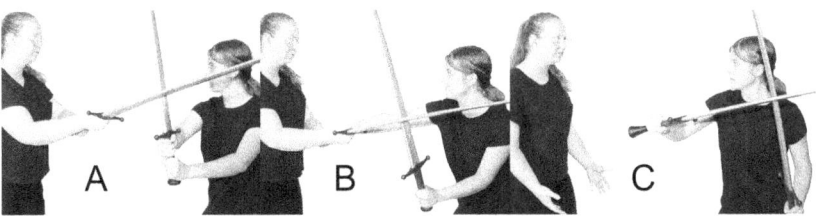

Figure 11.7 Grabbing the Sword Away

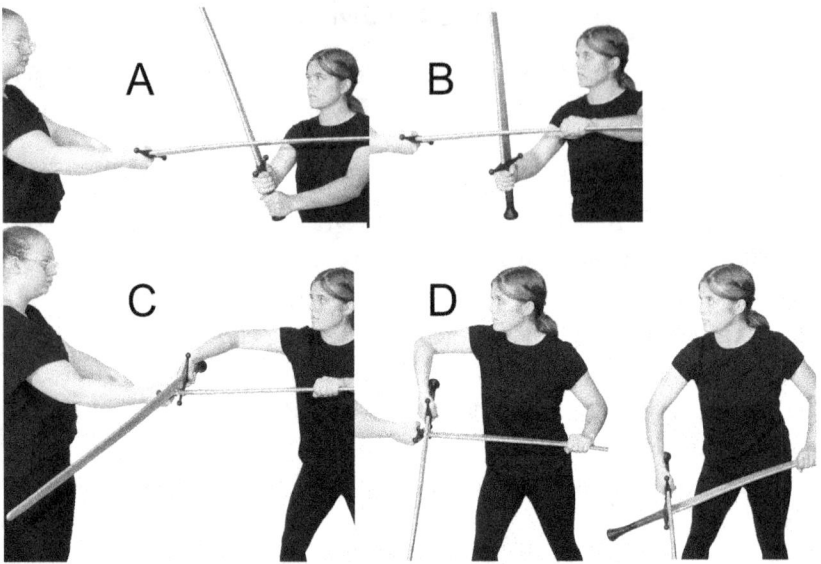

Figure 11.8 Leveraging the Sword Down

Leveraging the Sword Up

This starts in a high left bind (Figure 11.9a), A will reach over and grab the middle of B's blade (Figure 11.9b), A then lifts the hilt of their sword under the hilt of B's sword (Figure 11.9c), A pulls their hilt up toward them, pulling B's sword from their hand (Figure 11.9d). Be careful not to trap B's hand or fingers between the swords.

Variation

Both the leveraging disarms can be done from the half-sword position, the only change is removing the hand holding your blade and grab theirs.

Adding Flair

Now let's have some fun looking at actions that can add some flair to a fight. Are these moves practical? No. Are they historically accurate? Again, No. But are they fun, and add some excitement to a fight? Yes.

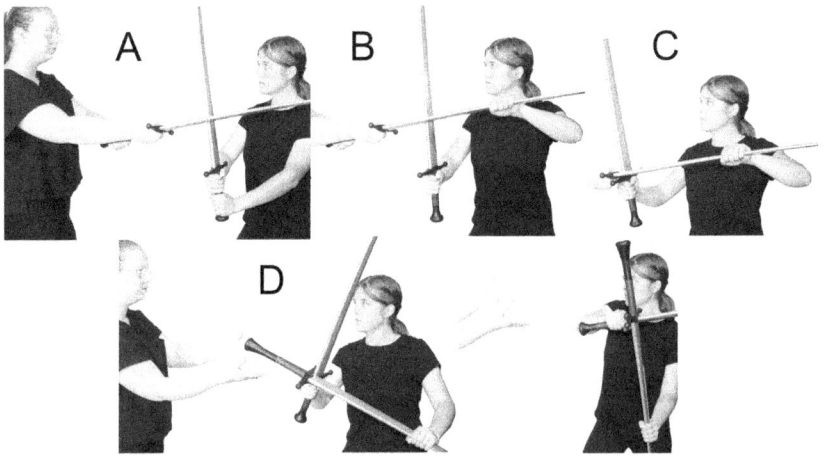

Figure 11.9 Leveraging the Sword Up

Sword Spins

Spinning the sword is fun. Spinning the sword looks "cool". Spinning the sword is totally impractical, but we see it all the time.

The easiest sword spin to do is a single-hand moulinet on one side. This is where you just roll the sword either forward or backward on your sword-hand side.

An advanced sword spin will be a double moulinet one on each side, creating the **Figure-8 Spin**. This starts with a forward roll from high right to low left, rolling up along the left side, then roll high left to low right. This can be repeated as many times as you want, ad infinitum.

A variation of the figure-8 spin is the "Conan" Spin – This comes straight from the film Conan the Barbarian (1982), where Arnold Schwarzenegger is doing a sword kata, and in that kata is a fun little spin. He draws out his sword, in a reverse grip, with the pinky toward the hilt and thumb toward the pommel. He then does a figure-8 spin in the reverse grip before doing a behind-the-back transfer to the left hand in a normal grip and does one rotation above his head.

Sword Flips

Again, a completely impractical action, but they can be awesome. Thirteen-year-old me was in awe of Madmartigan (Val Kilmer) when he did his sword flip in Willow (1988), and I have been fascinated and playing with swords ever since. Sword flips are not always easy, and it doesn't take much to mess one up and drop a sword, or to not get a good grip on it and send it flying off. Practice the action with a stick or synthetic sword before trying with a metal sword. And only add a flip to the choreography if the performer can perform it perfectly every time. A cool moment loses all credibility when the actor drops the sword by accident. If you are going to practice sword flips, be aware of the sword and your surroundings, and watch your feet! You will drop the sword several times. Also, be careful when trying to catch the sword, it's very easy for your hand to get in the way, or just the fingers.

The 180-flip just goes from either an underhanded grip to overhand grip, or vise versa. There are two ways to perform this: Forward or to the side.

To perform it forward, start in an underhanded grip, and using your wrist, flip the blade up and forward, while letting go of the handle, then once the tip is moving up, grab the handle again, you are now in an overhand grip.

To perform from the side, start in an underhanded grip, and using your wrist, flip the blade up and out, while letting go of the handle, then once the tip is moving up, grab the handle again, now in an overhand grip.

To make this a 360-flip, just give it a little more momentum and catch it back in the position it started in.

The Draw-Flip – Here, you will draw the sword out of the sheath with a reverse grip of the left hand, once the sword is unsheathed, do a 180-flip, and catch it in your right hand.

The Flat-Front Spin – This is a nice spin to add if you are looking for a little extra flair. In this spin, the sword will stay in front of the performer. With the blade flat, edges to the right and left, spin the sword clockwise, letting go with a little bit of a lift, let the sword do a full spin, and grab the handle again.

The Madmartigan Flip – this is a front flat spin flip. Start with right hand in overhand position on the handle, your left hand between you and your right hand. With the right hand in front of you, blade flat with your body, spin the sword clockwise and let go, then grab the sword with your left hand after ½ a turn, grabbing the sword in an underhanded grip, point down. Now continue rolling the sword the same direction and let go with a little bit of lift, this time the sword will do a full rotation, now grab the sword with your right hand while the point is down and allow the rotation to continue till your tip is up.

Spinning with a Sword

Another impractical action but can add some nice "dance-y" elements to a fight. Here, either the attacker or defender, or both if you really want it to have a dance quality to the fight, will spin around between actions. It can happen between attacks or parries. They can be moving forward or backward. It can even happen without directional movement.

Fire Swords

A great-looking effect is when a sword catches on fire, and there are specialty swords you can get that have blades made of Kevlar wick. However, whatever fuel you are using for the fire, as soon as the swords hit together, the fuel will go flying off in both directions, sending burning fuel everywhere. When you see practical fights in film where the swords are on fire, know that there are a lot of people off frame holding fire extinguishers and that they keep stopping and reapplying fuel. This is not something I recommend without proper supervision of a professional team.

Reversing Grips

Fighting with an underhand grip can add a quick element of energy to a fight, but in practicality is not very efficient.

Two-Sword Sword Fighting

Although this can be done with Hand-and-a-half swords, this is better suited for single-hand swords. However, if you want to show how proficient someone is with a sword, after they disarm one person, have them do a little bit of the choreography with a sword in each hand.

Physical Reactions to Pain

Finally, let us examine the physical reactions to the pain we have dealt out in the past couple of chapters. Remember, no matter how good an action looks, it is the reaction that sells it. When reacting to pain there are two rules to remember:

> Rule # 1 – That which gets hit first, moves first.
> Rule # 2 – The body will naturally go toward the pain.
> Bonus Rule # 3 – Pain doesn't magically disappear (unless you're a superhero or the main character who needs to keep fighting regardless of how much damage you have taken).

Move with the Hit

If you get hit in the face with a pommel, then your face/head needs to react first and follow the line of energy. When you get hit on the left side of your face, and the energy is moving straight across to your right, you need to move just your head and turn it to the right flat. Don't look up or look down during the turn, as that disrupts the line of energy. Only after your head has completely turned to the right, do you move your shoulders. Moving your shoulders at the same time as your head makes it look like you are a solid object and looks bad.

If the hit to the head comes from below, let the head tilt up first before engaging the rest of your body. The same is true if the hit is coming down, drop the head first, then let the body follow.

If you are getting hit in the stomach, the stomach moves in and the hips move back before the shoulders drop or the feet move.

If you are getting stabbed, turn toward the stab with the hips first, and then let the body follow.

Going Toward the Pain

The body will curl around the pain. If you get stabbed, after your hips turn with the action, allow your body to curl toward the pain. As the sword is pulled out, allow the hips to turn first and open out toward the pain.

If you are cut across the chest, pull your shoulders in, and if you are cut across the back, push your chest out.

When possible, always grab your injury afterward. This shows the audience where your pain is, and can either allow you to pop a blood pack or cover the fact that there is no hole in you or your costume.

Finally, if your character is injured in a fight, don't forget about it. Keep the limp or holding on to the pain from earlier. The more real your portrayal of the character in the fight, the more believable the fight will be for the audience.

Closing Comments

If you can get away with a noncontact action, use it. Only use contact actions when staging requires it. Performers can sell the action to the audience whether contact is made or not.

The victim, or receiver of the action, is always the one in control of the action.

Speeding up or adding extra force to an action does not help the scene, your partner, or the story.

We covered a lot of information in this short chapter. Take your time with the information and practice the application of techniques.

Be careful when performing killing actions and disarms. Pay close attention to distance and targets. Work everything slowly until fully capable of performing the actions without any mistakes or errors. Don't rush the learning process. It's better to take the extra time than to cause an injury.

Remember, it is always recommended to have a qualified fight director working with you on a production.

12

FINAL THOUGHTS FOR ACTORS AND DIRECTORS

Developing a fight is more than just slapping moves together. An analogy that was once told to me goes like this: "The moves are the raw ingredients of a great meal. It is about how you take them, prepare them, how they work together, and then finally how they are presented on a plate and served". Good choreography keeps everyone safe and serves the story, a superb and dynamic fight not only keeps everyone safe and serves the story but also builds the proper tension and excitement and draws a reaction from the audience.

In this last chapter of the book, we are going to explore the ideas and concepts that go into putting a finished fight together. In a perfect world, every theater show, no matter where they are located or how small the show or budget is, would have a skilled fight director putting the action together. Just as we wish every student or independent low-budget film would hire skilled stunt performers and a stunt coordinator. Unfortunately, that is not always the case, and we must move forward, but we must move forward safely. I hope that is what this section can do for you, whether you are a performer or director, I hope that the information contained in this closing chapter helps you become a better, safer performer or director. Please remember a book does not replace professional training or qualified fight direction.

So, what is it that goes into making a fight dynamic? For those answers, we are going to examine what I call the five elements of a dynamic fight: Physical Actions, Emotional Actions, Reactions, Vocal Actions, and Lines of Sight. Each of these works together to create an action sequence that will build tension, enhance the story, serve the characters, and keep the action safe and repeatable.

The Five Elements of Dynamic Fights

1. *Physical Actions*

    Every move the performer does is based on physical actions. However, choreography is more than just moving the weapon around in a safe fashion. The actor must utilize their entire training and employ full body acting. From breathing, body mechanics, footwork, offhand techniques, to facial expressions, the entire body of the actor must be utilized in telling the story and engaged in the performance.

    All too often, the actor can get so focused on the weapon work that they forget to move their body to match the energy being put into the choreography. Full body engagement keeps the story believable, and when these actions are developed at the beginning of the choreography training, they will be present at the performance. Like I stated in the beginning of the book, do not wait until the last minute to add these actions, make them part of the training and rehearsal process from the first day of rehearsal. As an actor, you must be aware of your total physicality while working on the actions. As a director, you need to remind your performers that a choreography is more than just the moves of the fight, it is all the actions from facial expressions, movements, breathing, and fighting techniques.

    Keep the feet active. Footwork is the base from which the actor moves. If your feet have no active movement, then the choreography has no active movement. Footwork can be used even in the tightest of spaces to increase the dynamic actions of the body. Proper footwork also keeps the actor safe in body alignment and moving across the stage. A dynamic choreography will utilize the whole body. As an actor, you need to keep your feet engaged in the action, paying attention to your stage and your surroundings, and staying in proper alignment with the moves. As a director, you need to make sure the fight moves around without a sense of disjointed actions, or danger from set pieces or other performers.

Add leans and avoidances. Not every action is going to land a hit, and that is a good thing. Narrowly escaping a move or using cunning to avoid an action builds the tension needed in a fight. If every action lands a hit, then it is either going to be a very quick fight, a very boring fight, or both. Move the body around and keep yourself active before, during, and after the action. Even if your character dies, the body is active after the hit, as you are moving to the floor, or as the character is struggling for life while dying slowly on stage. As actors, you need to pay attention to what your body is doing during the fight and the story it is telling. It is all too easy to want to be a badass fighter who never misses an action but asks yourself if that is really surviving the story your character needs to be telling. What level of energy should your character have in the moment? As directors, need to beware of the constantly bobbing performer. The physical energy needs to be directed into actions and not just nervous body energy. Remember, the moves must constantly support the character and the choreography. Fights should play out like a game of chess, where each fighter is assessing the other while trying to find the finishing move. A dynamic choreography utilizes levels of actions both connecting and missing.

Keep the actions concise. Sometimes, it is easy in theater to want to make the actions too big, or to allow the energy of the choreography to grossly exaggerate movements. Although there may be times we want that, such as in comedies or stylized actions, most of the time we want to keep the action believable and focused. As performers you will want to amplify the actions just enough so that the audience and your partner can keep up with the story, but if the actions are too exaggerated, the time it would take to set for the next action becomes disjointing, and the "danger to the character" aspect of the fight is lost. As a director, you will want to make sure the actions fit the scene and the story. You are the outside eyes for the performers and will help guide their actions to fit your vision and utilize actions that move the story forward and keeps the audience engaged.

Speed is your enemy. This is something you have read many times in this book, and I talked about at the start of the book. Take your time while learning the moves and the choreography. Once the moves are learned and you can perform the choreography all the way through with no mistakes, then you can start to speed the fight up to performance level. Your fight needs to move at the right pace. Too slow and it is boring, too fast and it looks unintentionally sloppy. As a performer, remember your tempo for the actions, as they will change throughout the choreography, do not rush yourself or your partner. Make each action clean and concise. As a director, focus on the rhythm of the choreography. Remember, the fight continues and enhances your vision and must remain a believable part of the world you have created. If the show is realistic or stylized, the fight must fit and that *dramatic convention* must be maintained.

Eyes help tell the story. Eye contact is important in the safety element of stage combat. When the actors are looking at each other, they are aware of their partner and working together. The eyes also help tell the emotional story of where the character focused and their state of mind. As a performer, if your character is unskilled and scared, you may be watching the attacks of the aggressor. If your character is skilled, you will focus more on your opponent and their full body actions. Even if you are playing characters who are scared, you will still need to keep checking in with your partner. This lets them know you are still engaged in the choreography and are ready for the actions. As a director, pay attention to the performer's focus, does it match their character and the emotional moment of the fight. Help guide them to establish focus when needed and keep the story being told.

Distance makes a difference. The space between the performers is just as important a part of the fight as the moves themselves. Expanding on what I spoke about at the beginning of the book, the use of distance can benefit or hamper a fight. If the actors are too close together, the audience cannot see the action, too far apart and the actions are unbelievable. As a performer, you need to be always aware of your distance. You will need to adjust and make alterations throughout the actions to maintain proper distance. As a director, you will need to help guide the performers, by letting them know when they are too close or too far away. Think of the story you are wanting the actors to tell and figure how distance may be a part of that story.

2. *Emotional Actions*

The emotional actions of a choreography are just as important as the physical actions. If our characters are not engaged in the fight emotionally, we are left with an empty feeling and have no attachment to the outcomes or consequences of the actions. Fights should always happen for a reason, and the consequences of the fight should be significant to the story and the characters, and without the actors portraying those emotions to us, it will fall flat.

The more out of control the character, the more in control the actor. If a character is enraged to the point of physical violence, the actor must characterize that rage in a controlled and repeatable manner. As a performer, you must take care to maintain the choreography. Do not let the tempo of the actions or the rhythm of the fight change just because you are feeling your character's emotions, or because your adrenaline is in full force during opening night. As a director, you will want to talk about the emotional elements in the choreography, walk through it, perform it slow with full emotion, and repeat as much as needed to develop the proper actions. Let the actors use their skills as performers in creating the emotion of the scene but keep the actions under control for safety and story. Talk to your actors about what expressions need to be used. Where the character is focused. Explore which emotion or emotions are driving the action forward. Why are the characters fighting? Is it revenge, anger, hate, frustration, fear, love, honor, self-preservation, or is the character showing off? Are they the ones instigating the actions or are they on the defensive? What is the emotion at the end of the fight? What are the consequences of winning or losing? How do the emotions change throughout the fight? It is important to have the performers and director talk about these questions before and during the work, as this will build a more dynamic choreography.

The emotions go beyond the actions. Very rarely does a fight just end. Even after the last action or killing blow, the emotion is still there. Fights are very rarely a standalone action. As a performer, ask yourself what my character's emotions are, and how do they change during the fight. As the director, it is your job to help the performers and provide those moments at the end of the fight.

3. *Reactions*

You can have the greatest moves ever written in a choreography, but one wrong, bad, or missing reaction will halt the audience's connection almost immediately. Reactions keep your story moving forward. They also help keep the audience believing actions that are happening, even when they know it is a staged fight. The suspension of disbelief will be maintained or lost by the quality of reactions from each performer in the fight. These reactions also fall onto other characters who may be onstage or in-frame during the scene.

Every action must have a reaction. This goes beyond the *action-reaction-action* technique of stage combat that I talked about in an earlier chapter. Here, we are talking about responses. The attack must be parried, blocked, avoided, or accepted. The emotional action of one character must have an emotional reaction from the other. Even the act of simply pulling out a sword must have a reaction from other actors on stage. If a character is injured, they must react appropriately, or inappropriately if it is a comedy. An example I love to use, and will later use when talking about vocal actions, is stubbing a toe. When you stub your toe, very rarely are you just going to look down and shrug your shoulders. We react physically by pulling our foot away from the offending object and usually end up holding the poor injured toes. We bring it into us. Just like if you were to accidently prick your finger with a needle or pin. We quickly pull our injured finger a way, usually clutching the hand in a fist. In these instances, an object is making a connection with part of our body, and our body's reaction to the pain is to move away from the pain. So too must this be done in a choreography. As a performer, ask yourself if you are acting or reacting. As a director, help the performers find the reactions, emotional or physical, to the actions happening around them and to them.

Physical reactions must follow the flow of energy. Here, we are talking about the flow of energy between the two combatants. Imagine watching a fight and a character throws a right hook, hitting the other character on the left side of the face, and the actor reacts by turning their head to their left. The *flow of energy* is disrupted by the incongruity of the reaction. If you are hit on the left, you should turn to your right. Now the audience may not immediately say to themselves, "oh the actor turned the wrong way", but they will have a mental disruption that will pull them from the fight. Another example where the reaction creates an undesired effect, a character gets lightly slapped in the face, the actor receiving the action overreacts by turning out with a big action and falls to the ground. If the purpose of the actions was to create a comic effect, then well done; however, if it was meant to build dramatic tension, the actions and reactions failed. As a performer, if your character is cut across their forearm, they must react with the injured body part in a way that follows the natural flow of energy (see previous section on "reacting to pain", in the Killing Actions and Adding Flair chapter). As a director, you need to keep watch and make sure that the flow of energy is in all the action and that the reactions match the story you are trying to tell.

The body is a solid object not a stiff object. One area where inexperienced fight performers struggle with is the separation of the physical actions of a reaction. An example of this is where a character is lightly hit in the face, and instead of just the head turning, the whole body turns as one reaction. As previously stated, this could be used for good comedic moments, but when trying to create a believable choreography, it disrupts the actions. There are over 300 joints in the human body. The part of the body hit first, reacts first. Let me repeat that – *the part of the body hit first, reacts first*. If a character is stabbed or cut in the arm, that arm moves first, followed by the shoulder, the upper body, then the other arm may come and hold/cover it. If a character is hit in the face, the head turns first, then the shoulders, then the back twists, then the hips, legs, and eventually the feet if the flow of energy requires it. If a character is avoiding a belly cut, the torso moves away from the object first, then the rest of the body follows. As a performer, you want to constantly be aware of your body movements and work to separate the physical actions. As a director, you will need to keep a keen eye on the physical movements of the performers and watch for any stiffness or lacking body reactions.

4. *Vocal Actions*

In the last of the actions category, we will examine the use of the voice in creating a dynamic fight. The voice gives us one of our "musical" elements of a fight. In film, this can be done in post-production, but on stage, it must be done live every time. Vocal actions fall both into the actions and reactions categories. They cover the range from energy and effort put forth, reactions to pain, reactions to emotions, and, of course, the dialogue of the scene. Vocalizations can be voluntary, involuntary, cathartic, exasperations, startling, intimidating, or controlled with the action. Not only do these sounds help create the excitement of a fight, but they also work to keep the performers properly breathing during the choreography.

A sound to the action. Without knaps or underscoring, the only sounds we get in a fight is the sound of the swords and combatants. It is important that we strike a balance with the vocalization. Too much and we sound like a Bruce Lee film, too little and we get nothing from it. As a performer, find the moments where you can punctuate a move with a sound, or can give vocalization to a block or avoidance. Try to find natural sounds early in the work, as what you rehearse is what you will perform. As a director, while setting the choreography play with different sounds, volumes, and inflections. Also, watch out for using "pow", "bang", or anything along those lines, if it is done during rehearsal, it will be done on stage.

If it cannot be seen, then it needs to be heard. Another skillful use of sound is as a vocal cue to your partner for an action happening that they cannot see. If you are performing an action behind your partner, a vocal cue, along with a touch cue, can allow them to react to the action. This also works if you are doing an action that the audience cannot see, such as a stab in the back with the victim facing the audience. As a performer, consider ways you can give vocal cues to your actions, both for your partner or for the audience. As director of the scene, make sure that both performers are giving a vocal cue when needed and be the audience's ears for the volume of vocalization.

Pain hurts, so let us hear it. A cut, a stab, the final death blow, all of these deserve a good sound reaction. They let the audience know something happened and lend a sense of realism to the fight. The level of severity of the injury, and the location, will alter the sound you make. Think of your sounds the same way you do in a hand-to-hand fight. The vocal scale of pain will match the action. Small cuts get a quicker, shaper sound, while stabs and deeper cuts have an exasperated deeper sound. Your death blows, however, will have a more guttural deep sound that may be sustained with your breath longer. Using variance in sounds relating to pain helps build variety and creates the music of a fight. As a performer, think about the different sounds you can make, play with them, and find what feels natural as a reaction. Directors should pay attention to the level of pain and the sound being produced. Help your performers discover the right sounds.

5. *Lines of Sight*

Lines of sight is where the sleight of hand and stage magic happen. The audience will believe what they cannot see. Utilizing the lines of sight allows the viewer to think actions are happening much closer in proximity than they are physically. This allows us to keep the actors safe while at the same time creating a dynamic and exciting fight. Understanding staging, the type of stage you are on, and where the audience is in relation to the action are factors that must be considered at every step of the choreography. Think of the fight as a game of show and tell. Some moves we will show to the audience; other we will tell with reactions as we hide the actual action. Below, we will examine the diverse types of ways we can manipulate these lines of sight.

Upstage/Downstage. The use of rotation in a fight will not only help in creating dynamic movement but also help in the selling of actions such as body cuts, quick thrusts, or other actions you do not wish the audience to see, especially regarding how far away the actual action is from the performer's body. This use of action is great for when the show is in a proscenium theatre style, or the audience only has one perspective on the fight.

In the round, move around. Performing fights in a space where the audience fully surrounds or mostly surrounds the stage can be tricky, spaces like thrust, black boxes, arena style theatres, or outdoor events. Here, the fight must move around and can add rotations during an action to hide the gap between actors. This does not mean that the fight must constantly circle around, as that would get very boring and repetitious to watch. However, using circular passes, or rotations at key moments in the choreography will help sell (and hide) the action. As performers, review your footwork and look for ways you can smooth the rotation of your actions. Directors can help by putting in off-line attacks, or avoidance that help move the fight.

5a. *Use of Implied Violence*

I must admit, this is my favorite kind of violence. Implied violence is where the action happens out of view from the audience. The audience's mind will imagine far worse than I can ever stage. A fight can move behind an object like a couch, and one actor can fall, as the other – from the audience point of view – stabs them repeatedly. This is a terrific way of creating a high amount of violence without having to show it. This also presents us a way to stage violence, without having to use blood effects. Now, there may be times you want the audience to fully see and experience the violence, but this is a great alternative to presenting violence that the audience cannot see, or you may be in a setting in which that level of violence is not needed to be seen. Another method of creating implied violence is by having the actors fight their way off stage or behind a large set piece, with only one actor returning, and depending on their time off stage, they can reenter covered in blood (think of Macbeth's death). As a performer, you must still perform with the same intensity and emotion with implied violence as you would with anything the audience can see. As a director, this is a wonderful way to create violence in a way that can tell the story without fully showing the actions. There are many ways to use implied violence, and I highly recommend utilizing it any chance you get, as it is just another tool in your box.

There are many components in which actors and directors can use to create an exciting and dynamic story on stage or in film, and these are just my personal five recommendations for actors and directors. There are terrific books on acting, action directing, fighting on film, and books about the art of fight directing and choreography. Never limit yourself to just one person's knowledge or point of view. I have created a list of highly recommended books in Appendix C that I hope you will check out.

Bruce Lee once said, "Adapt what is useful, reject what is useless, and add what is specifically your own." and I love that. Because in that quote he talks about developing your own martial style, and the same can be said about creating your unique theatrical combat style.

Be Safe, Be Dynamic, Be Entertaining.

GLOSSARY

Action(s): (a) Signifies an operation in its entirety, whether offensive or defensive. (b) Simple, compound, progressive, or combined movements of the weapon and/or body used to accomplish the combatant's objectives within a fight.

Active Block (also Active Parry): A defensive action that deflects or redirects the energy of the attack.

Active Hand: The non-weapon bearing hand used to *block, check, lock, parry, strike,* or *trap* the opposing weapon or parts of a partner's body, being kept active at chest level, and not hanging at the side of the body. Also known as *Alive Hand*.

Active Footwork: Footwork used to create dynamics within a fight.

Active Movement: Any movement executed in an augmented, more vibrant fashion.

Adjustment Step: (a) A small step intended to correct or realign the feet. (b) Any step that is not part of the choreography and is performed to fix a problem with distance or angle.

Advance: The leading foot steps forward, followed by the trailing foot, ending in the same distance between the feet as at the on-guard position (without crossing them). The opposite of *Retreat*.

Aggressor: See *Attacker*.

Alber (The Fool): One of the primary guards in German fighting systems. Similar to the Low Guard, with the tip pointing down.

The Archaeology of Weapons: Arms and Armor from Prehistory to the Age of Chivalry: A book published in 1960 by Ewart Oakeshott, where his classification of typologies first appeared.

Arm Block: A defensive action made with the hand or arm intended to stop a cut or thrust. A block can be made on either side of the body and in all lines.

Arming Sword: A single-handed sword used between 1000 and 1500c.e., with an average blade length of 30 in (75 cm)

Attack: (a) A simple or compound offensive action intended to harm one's opponent.

Attacker (also Aggressor, Operator): The actor/combatant who sets upon, attacks, or assails another; the one executing the violent action. The initiator of an offence action.

Avoidance: A defensive movement of the body.

Back: (a) The "back" or false edge of a blade. (b) The rear or dorsal part of the human body. Generally used in reference to the rear portion of the upper torso. (c) To go, or cause to go, backward or in reverse.

Back Edge: See False Edge

Backhand: The back of the hand.

Backpedal: To travel or move backward from an opponent through passing steps, or consecutive retreats, yet still facing them.

Basket Hilt: A type of hilt with by a basket-shaped guard that protects the whole hand.

Bastard Sword (also Hand-and-a-Half Sword): The common name for the Hand-and-a-Half sword, as it was a cross between the single handed sword, and the Two Handed sword.

Bastone: A stick or staff.

Behind-the-Back Block: Any block or parry performed behind the back of the defender.

Blade: The cutting edge of a tool or weapon.

Blade Flat: Also known as the Cheek or Face of a blade, refers to the widest flat sides of the blade.

Blade Point/Tip: The intersection of the front (edge) and back of the blade, intended for penetration or detailed cutting.

Blind Parry: A parry performed where the performer executing the parry cannot see the attack coming in, and relies on their partner to give a vocal cue for timing the connection at the intended target.

Block: A physical defensive action made with the body or weapon that hinders, checks, neutralizes, or nullifies an opponent's attack to stop it from reaching its intended target.

Blunt (also Rebated): (a) A bladed weapon without a sharp edge. (b) A practice weapon. (c) Adjective – not sharp.

Bind: (a) A checking action made on the opponent's weapon, executed by blocking the attack and then moving it diagonally to the opposite quadrant (i.e., from the inside high to the outside low, or outside high to inside low, etc.). (b) (also binden) The action of making contact between two weapons.

Binden: See Bind.

Boundary: Guideline that indicates or fixes a limit or extent to which an actor is willing to participate and establishes how others are able to behave around them and interact with them.

Broadsword: (a) A modern stage combat term used to refer to all hand-and-a-half swords. (b) A generic term for ship's cutlass, infantry sword, and heavy cavalry sabre.

Cadence: The rhythm in which a sequence of movements is made.

Casting: Directing the energy past your partner to prevent force going into them.

Ceding Parry: *See Yielding Parry.*

Central Ridge: The part of the swords blade. Swords with diamond cross-sections had a central ridge running along the middle of the blade just before the point, this helped strengthen the blade.

Center Line: The center of the body. Two imaginary lines that bisect the body into equal halves, both vertical and horizontal.

Cheat/Cheat in/Cheat out: To "cheat" is to turn your face or entire body either out to the audience (or camera) to be seen better without completely turning (so it still looks natural, but you are not completely in profile) or to face in to conceal something.

Circling Parry: Any parry or block that makes a circle before engaging with the incoming attack.

Claymore: (a) The Scottish variant of the late medieval two-handed sword (b) The Scottish variant of the basket-hilted sword.

Close: (a) The action of stepping inside measure, usually into an offensive action, to gain tactical advantage for both defensive and offensive actions. (b) To cover or shut a line of engagement against an attack. (c) To bring your feet together.

Closed Guard: A guard where there are no open lines of attack on the defender's body.

Closed Line: A line of engagement where the defender's weapon or other defensive object prevents an attack to that line of engagement or targeting.

Closing Distance: When performers move in toward each other, closing the distance between them, so that they may physically grab or manipulate the other performer.

Codex Wallerstein (also *Bauman Fechtbuch*): It is a German fencing manual compiled by Paulus Hector Mair in 1556.

Communication: The ability to communicate with a partner while staying in character, with theatrical believability and complete the set choreography.

Complex/Compound Footwork: An element of footwork that involve the execution of more than one simple component to complete the action.

Corps-à-corps (Body to Body): The act of two combatants closing distance to each other until they physically touch.

Counter: An act of prevention of an attack or move made against your opponent.

Counterattack: An attack made into an attack, either cut or thrust, which is intended to hit the opponent before the final movement of the opponent's attack is executed.

Croisé: A pris d'fer that moves the attacking weapon from a high to a low line, or low to high, on the same side of the body.

Cross-guard: The part of a sword's hilt, the bar that crosses the blade above the handle which protects the hands.

Cross Over (Forward and Back): A two-part movement consisting of two steps forward (or backward) in which the hips remain facing in the same direction on both parts of the move. This double step action ends in the same foot forward position as when it began.

Cross Step: An avoidance where the working leg crosses in front of the supporting leg (which stays in place or pivots on the ball of the foot), removing the combatant from the line of attack. A step that takes the body diagonally off-line to either the right or left, ending with the legs crossed.

Cue: An action said or done that provides a signal to a partner.

Cut: A stroke, blow, or attack made with the edge of a blade.

Cut Across the Head: A horizontal cut designed to look as if it will strike the head if it lands. It may travel right to left or vice versa and is usually avoided by ducking. Also called a "horizontal slash" to the head.

Cut Across the Stomach: A horizontal cut designed to look as if it would cut the stomach open if it landed. It may travel right to left or vice versa. The wrist is most often held to present the true edge and (for additional safety) the wrist/hilt lead with the butt/pommel of the weapon until the partners moves, at which point the cutting action is executed after it has passed the plane of the body. It is usually avoided by jumping back. Also called a "horizontal slash".

Cut to the Feet: A horizontal cut designed to appear to cut at the lower legs or feet and is avoided by jumping up to create the illusion of jumping "over" the attacking blade. The tip of the attacking blade is usually directed to a spot on the floor a few inches in front of the defender's feet.

Dao: A single-edged Chinese sword.

De Arte Gladiatoria Dimicandi: ("On the Art of Swordsmanship") is an Italian fencing manual by Philippo di Vadi, created between 1482 and 1487.

De Norske Vikingsverd: ("The Norwegian Viking Swords") is a book by Jan Peterson from 1919.

Defensive Guard: A stance where the non-dominant foot is forward.

Deflection: To cause something to change direction by interposing something; to turn aside from a straight course.

Deflective Parry: A parring action that deflects the incoming attack, rather than stopping it.

Deritto (Dritto, Dritti, Mandritto): An Italian term for Right-to-Left cuts on the horizontal.

Diagonal Cut or Slash with Avoidance: An off-line cut to either the inside or outside line. It may be a rising or a falling cut. It is usually avoided by leaning to the side away from the cut, with or without footwork.

Direct: An attack or riposte made in the line of engagement.

Disarm: The act of removing the partner's weapon by taking away a weapon or forcing the opponent to drop the weapon.

Disengage: To remove contact between weapons, the opposite of engage.

Distance: The proper measure between two or more performers to safely execute techniques in theatrical combat.

Out of Distance: The measure of distance where the attacker cannot make contact with their partner.

In Distance: The measure of distance where the attacker can make contact with their partner.

Displacement: See Thwart.

Dominant: The stronger or more controlled side. When right-handed the right side, when left-handed the left side.

Downstage: The front of a stage, or the closest part of a stage to the audience.

Double Edge: A blade with edges on both sides.

Draw Cuts: Cutting actions where the blade is in safe contact with the body and then drawn along the victim.

Duck: The vertical lowering of the body for the purpose of avoiding a cutting or a slashing action.

Dussack: A practice weapon with a broad curving blade and with a simple oval grip.

Edge: The Edge is the cutting surface of a blade that extends from point to shoulder/hilt.

Edge-to-Edge Parry: Any parry or block in which both weapons connect with their edges.

Engage: (a) The act of weapons touching. (b) To participate or become involved with.

En Guard: *See On Guard.*

Envelopment: A pris d'fer that carries the opponent's weapon around in a full circle, starting and ending in the same position

Emotional Actions: The representation of emotions created by the performer.

Estoc: A French sword, used from the 14th to the 17th century, with a cruciform hilt with a two-handed grip, a straight, edgeless, and sharply pointed blade.

Evasion: To avoid or escape an attack by moving the targeted area off the line of attack.

Extended Parry: A parry made with the arm in full extension.

Extension: The position or action during which a combatant reaches out with the limb, and if applicable body and/or weapon towards one's target.

Eye Contact: The means of two performers looking in their partner's eyes to assure mutual awareness and readiness to perform the techniques.

Expulsion: To throw off using the energy of the transport.

Fall: Safely descending with the illusion of being out of control.

False Attack: *See Feint Attack.*

False Edge: (a) A grind on the top of the blade, usually to allow a finer tip for better penetration. It can be very short or very long. (b) The edge of the blade opposite of the true edge on double-edged blades.

Fechtbuch (Plural Fechtbücher):   German term for Fightbook.

Feint Attack: An attacking action made without intending to hit and designed to either probe the opponent's defensive reaction or to draw a reaction or a parry.

Fehler: German for Feints, *see Feint Attack*

Fencing Master: A term used to denote expertise in the art of sword fighting.

Fendenti (Fendente):   An Italian term for downward cuts from either the right or left.

Fight Dynamics: Energy of movement, expressing intensity, accent, and quality.

Fight-Line: *See Line of Engagement.*

Figure-8 Spin: A spin that utilizes a double moulinet, one on each side of the body.

Fior di Battaglia (The Flower of Battle):   It is an Italian fencing manual authored by Fiore de'i Liberi around 1400.

Flank: Area of the body between mid-chest and the waist on either side.

Flat of the Blade: The flat, or wide part of a sword's blade.

Flat Parries: Parries or blocks executed with the flat or wide part of the blade. Opposite of an edge parry.

Flow of Energy: The direction in which effort is exerted through the body and through space.

Flyssa: An edged sword of Algeria.

Foible: The tip or weakest part of a sword blade, usually the top third of the blade.

Follow Through: Commitment to an action from beginning to end. To continue the cut or stab after the target has been struck, to the full extent of the blow.

Footwork: Activity or movement done with the feet.

Force: (a) The strength or energy as an attribute of physical action or movement. (b) To make someone do something against their will.

Fore Edge: *See True Edge.*

Forehand: (a) The palm of the hand. (b) The term used to indicate an attack, usually with the edge, delivered from the right if right-handed, from the left if left-handed.

Fore-Cut: A cutting attack with the fore or true edge of the blade.

Forte: The base or strongest part of a sword blade, usually the bottom third of the blade.

Froissement: *See Pressure Glide.*

Fuller: The grove in the sword blade, used to help strengthen the blade.

Gladiatoria: A German fencing manual created around the 1440s.

Glissade: A flowing attack on the blade performed from an already engaged position.

Goliath Fechtbuch: A German fencing manual created between 1535 and 1540, in the German tradition of Johannes Liechtenauer.

Grab: A holding, clasping, or seizure of any part of the opponent's body/clothing/weapon with the hand(s).

Grapple: To engage in close quarters fighting or struggling/to seize or hold.

Grasp: *See Hold.*

Grazing Strike: A hit with a body part or weapon that has the illusion of making contact, and then following through its target.

Grip: (a) The part of the handle normally held by the hand. (b) The manner in which the weapon is held.

Grounding: Having a stable base from which to perform fight choreography.

Guard: (a) The portion of the hilt between the blade and the grip that protects the hand. (b) A posture of defense.

Gründtliche Beschreibung, der freyen Ritterlichen unnd Adelichen kunst des Fechtens, in allerley gebreuchlichen Wehren, mit vil schönen und nützlichen Figuren gezieret und fürgestellet: ("A Thorough Description of the Free, Chivalric, and Noble Art of Fencing, Showing Various Customary Defenses, Affected and Put Forth with Many Handsome and Useful Drawings") a German fencing manual created by Joachim Meyer in 1570.

Half Pass: A simple form of footwork that carries the foot forward or backward in the same manner as a pass, only bringing the foot to rest next to the opposing foot rather than one foot length past it.

Half Pronation/Supination (also Middle or Vertical Position): The placement of the weapon bearing hand where the thumb is held at roughly 12 o'clock (Half Pronation) or 6 o'clock (Half Supination).

Half Sword: A technique where one hand holds the handle, and the other hand holds onto the blade. This can be used in both defensive and offensive actions.

Hammer Grip (also Fist Grip): The most basic of all grips and is achieved by grabbing the handle of the weapon, wrapping your fingers around the grip, and allowing the thumb to wrap over the index finger.

Hand-and-a-Half Sword (also Bastard Sword): A sword with a double-edged blade, with a handle longer than a single hand sword, but not as long as a two-handed sword. Usually handles would be 7–10 in (17–25 cm).

Handle: The handle of a sword is the portion you grip. Also, see Grip.

Hanging Guard: A guard at or above head level, with the blade held parallel to the ground or at an angle lower than the hilt.

Hanging Parry: Any parry or block made above the waist in a high line, where the hilt is higher than the tip of the sword.

Heel: The heel of the blade refers to the section of the blade next to the guard or handle.

Hero's Parry: A variation of the hanging parry with the addition of a displacement away, creating a sloping of both body and blade.

High Guard: A guard at or above head level.

High Lines: The areas of the body above the waist.

Hilt: The part of a sword containing the guard, handle, and pommel.

Hilt Bash/Strike: An attack with the hilt of the sword.

Hit: An offensive action which lands with point or edge on the target. An attack that successfully lands, or appears to land, with point or edge on the target.

Hold (also Grasp): To use one or both hands for clutching or grasping the opponent.

Horizontal Attack: Any cutting attack that travels in a plane parallel to the floor.

Hunch: The physical act of raising one's shoulders towards the head and bending the top of the body forward.

Hunting Sword: A single-hand short sword.

Hyperextend: To go beyond the natural range of motion for a joint or part of the body moving about a joint. To extend in the sense opposite to flex, so as to attain an abnormally great angle.

Implied Violence: Violence that is not seen by the audience and is only suggested or implied by the actor's physical actions viewable or heard by the audience.

In Distance: The measure where combatants could make contact with their partner by extending their weapon.

In Fighting: (a) When two combatants have closed distance and are inside normal measure. (b) The practice of moving inside fighting measure, getting up close to one's opponent to deliver a blow with the hand or hilt of a weapon. (c) Fighting at close quarters, hand to hand.

In Line: See On-Line.

Indirect: An attack or riposte made in another line. An attack not delivered in the line of engagement.

Inside Block: A block used to deflect straight or circular strikes directed at the head or midsection on your inside line.

Inside Line: (a) The area of attack and defense on a combatant, delineated by their vertical center line, which is furthest from their weapon bearing side. Opposite of Outside Line. (b) The lines or parry positions protecting the side of the body farthest from the sword-arm.

Intention: (a) The direction of focus. (b) The wants/needs of the character.

Isolation: The ability to move or maneuver a specific part or parts of the body independent of the others.

Jump: A footwork action, either forward, backward, or up, where both feet leave the ground simultaneously.

Kasskara: A sword with strait guard and disk-shaped pommel, typical of the Sudan and Sahara region.

Katana: A Japanese sword.

Khepesh: An Egyptian sickle-shaped sword.

Knap: The act of making the sound of a hit.

Knee Attack: Any attack giving the illusion of contact with the knee.

Knife: An offensive and defensive weapon or tool consisting of a blade with a sharpened longitudinal edge fixed in the handle, either rigidly or with a joint, or clap-knife. The blade is generally of steel.

Knock-Away Parry: Any parry or block that attacks the blade of the incoming weapon and knocks it away from the intended target or path.

Krumphau: One of Liechtenauer's Master Strikes, the Krumphau, or Twisted strike, goes from the right of the attacker to the right of the defender.

Lag/Back: The part of the body that is behind the others.

Lag Foot: *See trailing foot.*

Lead/Front: The part of the body that is ahead of the others.

Left Dominant: To have more control in, or to be more dexterous with the left hand.

Liberi, Fiore de'i: (Fiore Furlano de'i Liberi de Cividale d'Austria 1381–1409) was a late 14th century knight, diplomat, and fencing master. Author of Fior Di Battaglia.

Liechtenauer, Johannes: A fencing master from Germany, attributed author of Zettel. A major influence in the German school of sword fighting.

Lifting Cut: A lifting cut performed with the false edge that curves out then back in during the action.

Linear Footwork: The practice of moving or working actions of the feet in straight lines rather than in circular planes.

Lines of Attack or Defense: Referring to the imaginary planes that bisect the body into four equal sections, one vertical (delineating Inside and Outside) and one horizontal (delineating High and Low). The line may be open or closed, according to the relationship of the attacking blade, the target, and the defending blade.

Line of Engagement: The line between fighters in which the weapons and their bodies are aligned and threatening.

Lines of Sight: The lines along which an audience or viewers see the action.

Line of Direction: Also known as a fight line, this is an imaginary line between two combatants/performers that represents the line of engagement.

London and the Vikings: A book by Sir Mortimer Wheeler, published in 1927.

Long Guard: A guard position where the arms and sword are extended fully away from the body.

Longshield: A large shield used for dueling.

Low Guard: A guard in front of the body and below the shoulders, with the blade held with the tip directed down.

Mair, Paulus Hector (1517–1579): A German fencing master who collected and published several works throughout his life.

Marozzo, Achille (1484–1553): An Italian Fencing Master, best known for his book Opera Nova (New Work), published in 1536.

Masking: The action of "hiding" combat techniques from the audience, to create the illusion of realism.

Measure: The distance between combatants when on guard, determined by the length or reach of the fighters and their weapons.

Measure of a Step: The distance by which one foot moves forward in front of the other one.

Meisterhau: "Master strikes", this term is used in reference to Liechtenauer's five master cuts: Zornhau, Krumphau, Zwerchhau, Schielhau, and Scheitelhau.

Messer: (also Grosse Messer) meaning "long knife", this sword has short, single-edged blade which is slightly curved at the end, and the last few inches of the clipped back is sharp.

Meter: A systematically arranged and measured rhythm for movement.

Method of Action (also known as Action-Reaction-Action, Action-Reaction-Completion, Cue-Reaction-Action, or Preparation-Reaction-Action): The process of actions in theatrical combat and of communicating with a partner during a choreography, while staying in character and maintaining a safe performance.

Meyer, Joachim (1537–1571): A German fencing master, best known for his work Gründtliche Beschreibung, der freyen Ritterlichen unnd Adelichen kunst des Fechtens, in allerley gebreuchlichen Wehren, mit vil schönen und *nützlichen Figuren gezieret und fürgestellet* ("A Thorough Description of the Free, Chivalric, and Noble Art of Fencing, Showing Various Customary Defenses, Affected and Put Forth with Many Handsome and Useful Drawings").

Mezani (Mezzane): An Italian term for all horizontal cuts.

Middle Guard: A guard in front of the body and below the shoulders, with the blade held with the tip directed up.

Mittelhau: A German term for the horizontal cuts, from either the left or the right.

Mortuary Hilt Sword: A later development of the Basket Hilt Sword of the 17th century.

Moulinet (Molinello): An action with the sword where it moves in a circle on the horizontal, vertical, or horizontal plane.

Neutral Position: The neutral position is the bodily posture in which a performer is standing with the feet slightly apart and under the hips and shoulders with neither foot in the lead. The arms are hanging relaxed to each side of the body and the thumbs point forward.

Non-Dominant: The weaker or less controlled side. Opposite of dominant. When right-handed the left side, when left-handed the right side.

Nebenhut (Near Ward): One of the secondary guards in German fighting systems. Similar to the Tail Guard, with the tip pointing low and with the tip pointing back behind the fighter.

Oakeshott, Ewart (1916–2002): A British historian, author, and illustrator. He created the Oakeshott Typology.

The Oakeshott Typology: Created by Ewart Oakeshott, this typology is used to define and catalog the various swords of the 11th through 16th centuries in Europe based upon their physical characteristics.

Oberhau: A German term for all downward cuts, either vertical or diagonal.

Ochs (Ox): One of the primary guards in German fighting systems. Similar to the Hanging Guard, with the tip pointing forward, the blade held parallel to the ground or at an angle lower than the hilt.

Off/Open/Check-Hand: The non-weapon bearing hand.

Off-Line (also Offline): (a) Any attack that is directed to a target away from the body. (b) The relationship of combatants' bodies when the center lines of the combatants are offset. (Off Target) (c) Any action consisting of taking the body or weapon off the line of engagement.

Off-Line Step: Any movement that takes the body away from the Line of Engagement.

Off-Set (also Offset): Where the centerline of two combatants facing one another does not line up. One combatant is cheated to one side or the other. *See also Off-Line.*

On-Guard: The ready position from which a person can launch an offensive or defensive movement.

On-Line (also Online): (a) A mode of theatrical fighting where attacks are aimed at specific body targets on the combatant. (b) The position of the two partners' bodies where the shoulders are precisely lined up, no matter where they are on stage. (c) Any action consisting of keeping the body or weapon on the line of engagement.

On-Line Attack (also on Target): (a) An attack made directly to a target area of the body.

Open: (a) The area on one's opponent that is unprotected. (b) An action to increase distance between combatants, or to move your feet apart.

Open Guard: A guard where there are open lines of attack on the defender's body.

Opening: An unguarded area.

Opera Nova (New Work): An Italian fight book, published in 1536 by Achille Marozzo.

Out of Distance: The measure where combatants could not make contact with their partner by extending their weapon.

Outside Block: (a) A block made on the outside or backside of the attacking hand arm, or leg. (b) A defensive action made on the same side of the body, generally made on the outside or backside of the defending hand or arm.

Outside Lines: The parts of the target on the side nearest to the sword arm. The parts of the body to the dominant side (right of the sword hand when one is right-handed and left of the sword hand if one is left-handed).

Overarm: The tip of the weapon facing up above the thumb when held.

Overhand Grip: Holding a sword with the point above the hand. Opposite of Underhand Grip.

Parry: A defensive action of blocking an incoming attack.

Parry 2: A defensive block made with the sword, protecting the low inside line.

Parry 3: A defensive block made with the sword, protecting the high inside line.

Parry 4: A defensive block made with the sword, protecting the high outside line.

Parry 5: A defensive block made with the sword, protecting the high outside line, hilt on your high inside line.

Parry 5a: A defensive block made with the sword, protecting the high inside line, hilt on your high outside line.

Parry 7: A defensive block made with the sword, protecting the low outside line.

Partner: For the purposes of staged combat, all techniques both in attack and defense are worked in partnership. Not in competition with a fellow actor.

Partnering: A process in which two or more combatants actively work together to safely and effectively make nonviolent actions appear real and dangerous.

Pass: A movement that takes the body in a straight line forward or backward by passing the foot and changing the lead foot (the foot in the front or forward position of the stance).

Pass Backward: A linear step backward made by passing the lead foot to the rear. Opposite of the Pass Forward.

Pass Forward: The trailing foot crosses the leading foot to the fore one full step. Hips may or may not retain original orientation. Opposite of Pass Back.

Pass Through: To move an object through the targeted zone.

Peen Block: A metal block between the peen and the pommel.

Petersen, Jan: Author of *De Norske Vikingsverd* (1919), and historian who listed 26 types and subtypes of Viking swords.

Pflug (Plow): One of the primary guards in German fighting systems. Similar to the Low Guard, with the tip pointing down.

Phrase: A section of fight choreography. An exchange of blade patterns and body movements that often ends with a choreographed punctuated pause. (E.g., end in a corps a corps, a wound or kill, a break in the action, etc.)

Physical Actions: The actions created with the body by the performer.

Pisano, Philippo di Vadi (1425–1501): An Italian fencing master and author of *De Arte Gladitoria Dimicandi* (On the Art of Swordsmanship).

Pivot: (a) The act of swinging or turning the body while keeping the center of gravity fixed at a central point. (b) A shifting of the foot on either the ball or heel.

Pommel: A conical or disk-shaped piece of metal located at the rear of the grip which serves the dual purpose of locking the different parts of the weapon together and acting as a counterweight to the blade.

Pommel Attack: Any aggressive or offensive action, usually in close distance, delivered with the pommel of a weapon.

Point: (a) See Blade Point. (b) To direct attention toward something/someone by extending a finger or object held in the hand.

Posta: The Italian term for guard positions. The 12 common guards are below:

1. **Posta frontale ditta corona** (crown guard)
2. **Posta di finestro** (window guard)
3. **Posta breve** (short guard)
4. **Tutta porta di ferro** (whole iron door)
5. **Posta di donna** (woman's guard)
6. **Posta di donna la sinestra** (woman's guard on the left)
7. **Posta longa** (long guard)
8. **Porta di ferro mezana** (middle iron door)
9. **Dente di zenghiaro** (boar's tooth)
10. **Posta di bicorno** (two horned guard)
11. **Posta di dente zenchiaro mezana** (middle boar's tooth guard)
12. **Posta di Coda lunga** (long lying tail)

Press: An attack on the blade where it is pushed offline to open an area of attack.

Pressure Attack: An attack on the blade where constant pressure is used to control or displace the blade.

Pressure Glide: An attack on the blade where the controlling blade pushes forcefully down from the foible to the forte of the opposing blade.

Pris d'fer: Any controlling attack on the blade.

Pronation: The position of the hand where the palm is turned down.

Reaction: An action performed, or a feeling experienced in response to a situation or event.
Ready Stance: A relaxed stance from which offensive and defensive actions can instantly and equally be made.
Rear Foot: *See Lag Foot.*
Recover: Returning to a guard position.
Redirection: An action where the hand or arm intercepts the attack and then immediately displaces or removes the threat by controlling the energy away.
Reinforced Block/Parry: Any block or parry where additional support, either with a hand or other weapon/prop, is used to support the defending weapon.
Rest: A noticeable pause in action or movement.
Retreat: An action in the footwork that carries the body backward by moving the rear foot first and then the lead foot (without crossing them). Opposite of Advance.
Reverse Grip: (a) An underarm Hammer or Fist grip achieved by grabbing the handle of the weapon, tip facing down, wrapping your fingers around the grip, and allowing the thumb to wrap over the index finger. (b) An underhand grip on a weapon.
Ridoppio: An Italian term for rising diagonal cuts.
Riverso (Riversi, Roversi): An Italian term for Left-to-Right cuts.
Rhythm: (a) The visible and audible variables of rate within beats and phrases of a fight. (b) The temporal pattern produced by the grouping and balance, or imbalance and unpredictability, of sounds and dialogue during a fight. The strong and weak elements in the flow of sound and silence.
Right Dominant: (a) Having the right hand and/or foot forward in an on guard or ready stance. Generally referring to the lead foot in the on-guard stance. (b) To have more control in, or to be more dexterous with the right hand.
Rising Block: (a) A block delivered upward to defend against a descending diagonal or vertical attack. (b) A deflection block, made with either arm, which protects the head.
Rocking: (a) The back-and-forth movement of the body during the execution of stationary footwork. (b) In active footwork; a partial advance or

retreat (traveling about ½ the distance of a standard footwork) on the part of the combatants.

Rotation: The act of turning or rotating a limb (wrist, hand, head, arm, leg, etc.), the body, a weapon, or other object, in one direction or another. To turn circle-wise.

Scheitelhau: "Parting Strike" – Outreaching the low line attack from your partner by extending your attack on the high line.

Schielhau: "Squinter" – A hooked strike from high with the false edge.

Sharp: To have a keen edge or point; being well suited for cutting or piercing; a blade tapered to a fine edge or point; opposite to blunt.

Sheath: The case, covering, home, or lodging for the blade of a weapon when not in use; usually close fitting and conforming to the shape of the blade, the blade is generally thrust into the sheath by way of an opening at its top.

Short Guard: A guard term for when the sword and arms are held closer to the body.

Shove: A strong or violent thrust or push with the feet, hands, or body, quickly moving a body away from the agent.

Sidestep Evasion: Evasive actions that remove the body from the cutting plane of a diagonal or vertical swipe by lunging either to the left or to the right and leaning the torso into the lunge, creating, with the body, a parallel plane to the attack outside the cutting plane.

Simple Footwork: A base element of footwork that involves the execution of one component.

Slash: *See Swipe.*

Slit: To cut.

Sloped Parry: *See Hero's Parry.*

Small Step: An advance or retreat that is more a shuffle than a proper step.

Sottani (Sotano): An Italian term for an upward cut from either the right or left.

Spatial Awareness: The state of being aware of your surroundings and your position relative to them.

Speed: The velocity or rate at which a fight is moving. The degree of quickness of movement, both of weapon and body, usually as a result of exertion, clarity, swiftness; also, the power of rate of progress.

Squalembrato: An Italian term for descending diagonal cuts.

Stab: (a) To drive, to plunge, to thrust, or kill with the point of a weapon. (b) To make or offer a thrust with the point of a weapon.

Stance: The specific positioning of the feet and body as part of correct physical placement for a particular technique or form of combat.

Static Block: A defensive action that stops the attack. The defender's action is held in place, and the movement of the action comes to a complete stop.

Step: An action of footwork where the foot moves a normal distance, measured by the stride of your natural walk.

Exaggerated Step: A step larger than your normal stepping distance.

Half Step: An action of footwork where the foot moves half the distance of your natural walking step.

Micro Step: An action of footwork where your foot moves forward or backward only a few inches.

Passing Step/Crossover Step: Simple action of footwork that moves a combatant forward or backward by passing their lead foot to the rear beyond their lag foot into a new lag position, or by passing their lag foot to the front beyond their lead foot into a new lead position.

Slide Step: A step that moves the foot by sliding instead of a lift and place.

Shuffle Step: A move that requires both feet to slide step.

Stop Short: A term used to describe a false attack where the performer prepares for a cut, begins the first action, then immediately goes back into a different guard.

Striking Parry: A parry that strikes the incoming action from behind the momentum and forces it to continue on its path.

Straight Attack: An attack executed from an open guard position directly toward an opponent without changing the line of engagement.

Style: (a) A personal or characteristic manner of executing a fight. (b) An aesthetic and creative choice based on the actual mechanics of the weapon or form of combat.

Supination: The position of the hand when the palm is turned up.

Swipe: An exaggerated cutting action that passes through the target area without contact.

Belly Swipe: An exaggerated cutting action giving the impression it is targeting the belly.

Foot Swipe: An exaggerated cutting action giving the impression it is targeting the feet/legs.

Head Swipe: An exaggerated cutting action giving the impression it is targeting the head.

Tail Guard: A guard at the side of the body, at or below the waist, with the blade held with the hilt forward and the tip directed back.

Takes: In film or television – a scene or sequence of sound or vision photographed or recorded continuously at one time.

Takouba: A sword used among the western Sahel, usually measuring one meter in length.

Talhoffer, Hans: A 15th-century fencing master from Germany, author of multiple manuscripts.

Tang: The base of a sword blade that the hilt, handle, and pommel attach to.

Target: The part of the body towards which an attack is directed.

Technique: A term for a specific move or action; especially in martial arts.

Tempo: The pace or speed at which an action happens.

Thrust: An attack made with the point of the weapon. See also Stab.

Thwart: A step that takes the body diagonally offline to either the right or left, ending with the legs open. Also a Displacement.

Thumbing the Blade: The act of placing the thumb under the sword and against the flat of a blade at the cross guard to allow better control of the tip.

Timing: (a) The synchronization of each action and its corresponding reaction throughout a fight; the coordination of which incorporates both the speed at which actions are performed as well as the action-reaction speed of intrinsic partnered movements. (b) To acknowledge an opportunity or opening and execute the correct action at the best possible moment.

Training Sword: Training swords are any sword designed for use as a training aid. The blades are blunt, usually of aluminum, rubber, wood, or synthetic resin, with rounded and blunted tips.

Transfer Block: See *Replacement Block*.

Transition: (a) A movement of the blade from one line to another. (b) To change from one action or guard to another.

Transport: A checking action made on the opponent's sword, executed by blocking the attack and then moving it vertically from a high line to a low line, or vice versa, but on the same side as the block took place.

Trap: An act or action that immobilizes an opponent's limb(s) and or weapon to affect an attack or disarm.

Traverse: A movement that takes the body in a straight line right or left and maintains the lead foot. These are used to either take the performer offline from an attack or used to maintain the fighting line during an attack.

True Edge: The edge of the double-edged blade that is aligned with the middle-knuckles (the joint between the Proximal and Intermediate phalanges) of the hand holding it. On single edge blades, it is the only edge.

Turn-in: The rotation of the leg at the hips which causes the feet (and knees) to turn inward, toward the front of the body.

Turn-out: The rotation of the leg at the hips which causes the feet (and knees) to turn outward, away from the front of the body. This rotation allows for greater extension of the leg, especially when raising it to the side and rear.

Unarmed: Without weapons.

Underarm: The tip of the weapon facing down below the little finger when held.

Underhand Grip (also Ice Pick Grip and Reversed Grip): A way of holding a weapon with the blade held beneath the hand (gripped with the thumb at the pommel) and managed as a stabbing weapon. Opposite of Overhand Grip.

Unterhau (Under Cut): A German term for rising and upward cuts.

Upstage: The back of the acting area, or the furthest part of the stage away from the audience.

Upward Block: Any one of numerous blocks used to neutralize an opponent's high-line attack.

Vertical Attack: Any cutting attack that travels from a high line to a low line, or vice versa, in a plane that is perpendicular to the floor.

Victim Control: In theatrical combat, the actions of the choreography are controlled by the "victim" (the one who is having the violence acted upon them).

Victim (also Recipient): The actor/combatant on the receiving end of any given attack. The recipient of an offensive action.

Violence: The exercise of physical force (whether intentional or unintentional, armed or unarmed) so as to inflict injury on, or cause damage to, persons or property; or forcibly interfering with personal freedom.

Violent: (a) Having some quality or qualities in such a degree as to produce a very marked or powerful effect (esp. in the way of injury or discomfort). (b) Intense, vehement, very strong, or severe.

Vocal Cue: In theatrical combat, a sound is used to notify a scene partner of an upcoming or imminent action.

Vocal Reaction: A sound performed in reaction to an action delivered to or from a performer.

Volanti: An Italian term, primarily used by Vadi, refereeing to horizontal cuts.

Vom Tag (Dach/Tach/Tage) (From the Roof): One of the primary guards in German fighting systems. Similar to the High Guard.

Walk-Through: A slow rehearsal speed/pace.

Ward: See Guard.

Waterfall Parry: *See Hero's Parry.*

Weapon Bearing Side: The side of the body that brandishes or carries the weapon.

Wheeler, Sir Mortimer (10 September 1890–22 July 1976): He was a British archaeologist and officer in the British Army.

Wield: To use with the hand, to manage weapons.

Wilhalm, Jörg: A German fencing master who produced several manuscripts in the later 1400s and early 1500s.

Winding (Winden): A German fencing term referring to the action where the sword turns along the opponent's weapon during a bind. It is used to gain leverage and change the angle of attack to find open targets without losing an advantage.

Wrapping the Finger: A technique where the dominant hand will wrap the index finger up and over the cross guard of the sword.

Yield: (a) To give up or surrender; the action of giving in; submission. (b) To deliver, to render, to give up, to surrender. (c) To give way, to succumb.

Yielding Parry (Ceding): A perry against a flowing attack, performed without disengaging or separating the blades.

Zettel (Recital): A long poem of rhyming couplets which have been ascribed to Johannes Liechtenauer.

Zones of Attack/Defense: Areas of the body the performers target or defend. Defined in four zones:

High Inside: This target zone is from the waist to the head, on the non-weapon baring side.

High Outside: This target zone is from the waist to the head, on the weapon baring side.

Low Inside: This target zone is from the waist to the head, on the non-weapon baring side.

Low Outside: This target zone is from the waist to the feet, on the weapon baring side.

Zornhau: "Strike of Wrath" – A high right diagonal attack.

Zwerchhau: "Cross Strike" – False edge attack to partners left side, true edge for right side.

Zwehandler: A German term for a two-handed sword.

APPENDIX A
ORGANIZATIONS

Academy of Performance Combat (A.P.C.) / theapc.org.uk
Academy of Dramatic Combat / academyofdramaticcombat.com
Academy of Theatrical Combat / theatricalcombat.com
Actors' Equity Association (AEA) / actorsequity.org
American Entertainment Armouries Association (AEAA) / aeaa.us
American Guild of Musical Artists (AGMA) / musicalartists.org
Art of Combat International / artofcombat.org
British Academy of Dramatic Combat (B.A.D.C.) / badc.org.uk
British Academy of Stage and Screen Combat (B.A.S.S.C.) / bassc.org
Davenriche European Martial Artes School / swordfightingschool.com
Dueling Arts International / duelingarts.com
Fight Directors Canada (F.D.C.) / fdc.ca
FightRight (Northern Ireland) / fightright.org.uk
HEMA Alliance / hemaalliance.com
Humble Warrior Movement Arts / humblewarriormovement.com
International Alliance of Theatrical Stage Employees, Moving Picture Technicians, Artists and Allied Crafts of the United States (IATSE) / iatse.net

Intimacy Coordinators Canada / intimacycoordinatorscanada.com
Intimacy Directors & Coordinators (IDC) / idcprofessionals.com/
Intimacy Professionals Association (IPA) / intimacyprofessionalsassociation.com
Moving Body Arts (UK & EU) / movingbodyarts.com
New York Combat for Stage & Screen / nycstagecombat.com/
Nordic Stage Fight Society / nordicstaegfight.com
Rapier Wit / rapierwit.com
RC-Annie Ltd. / rc-annie.com
Screen Actors Guild and the American Federation of Television and Radio Artists (SAG-AFTRA) / sagaftra.org
Society of American Fight Directors (S.A.F.D.) / safd.org
Society of Australian Fight Directors Inc. (S.A.F.D.I.) / safdi.org.au
Stage Directors and Choreographers Society (SDC) / sdcweb.org
Theatrical Intimacy Education (TIE) / theatricalintimacyed.com

APPENDIX B
SUPPLIERS

Sword & Weapons

Baltimore Knife and Sword Co. / baltimoreknife.com (a good rental house)
CAS Iberia / casiberia.com (a nice selection)
Century Martial Arts / centurymartialarts.com (good source for martial arts supplies)
Cold Steel / coldsteel.com (great quality, wonderful synthetic weapons)
Creations (formally known as Starfire Swords) / starfireswords.com (the weapon of the Renaissance Faire world)
Cuchilleria Albacete / cuchilleriaalbacete.com (great source for true Navajas)
Fight Designer LLC / fightdesigner.com (a personal friend, a good selection of weapons, and an amazing selection of firearms)
Forte Stage Combat / fortecombat.com (a good rental house)
Keen Edge Knives / keenedgeknives.com (training, prop, and specialty knifes and daggers)

Macdonald Armouries / macdonaldarms.com (custom weapons from an amazing artist and historian)
Museum Replicas Limited / museumreplicas.com (a decent selection)
Preferred Arms / preferredarms.com (rental house for film and theatre)
Purpleheart Armory / woodenswords.com (great Texas owned business, lots of options)
RC-Annie / rc-annie.com (great supply of rentals for the UK and EU)
Rogue Steel / roguesteel.com (custom, rental, repairs, with a good selection)
Street Forge Armory / bit.ly/streetforgearmoury (great owners and creators, esp. of African weapons) (contact the owners for custom work. All their work is high quality)
Weapons of Choice / weaponsofchoice.com (a major national rental house for stage weapons)
Therion Arms / therionarms.com (a retailer of historical, theatrical, and display arms and armor)

Fire Swords

Dark Monk / dark-monk.com/
Trick Concepts / trickconcepts.com/fire/swords/
Fire Toys / firetoys.com/fire/fire-equipment/fire-swords.html
Juggling Wholesale / jugglingwholesale.com/flow-arts/fire-dancing-equipment/fire-sword

APPENDIX C
ADDITIONAL RESOURCES

Books on Theatrical Combat

Academy of Theatrical Combat Basics Level 1 – by Dan Speaker, Jan Bryant, et al.
Acted Aggression – by Kara Wooten
Actors on Guard – by Dale Anthony Girard
The Art of Knife Fighting for Stage and Screen – by Erick Wolfe (yup, that's my other book)
The Art of Unarmed Stage Combat – by Robert Najarian
Basics of Stage Combat: Single Sword – by Andrew Ashenden
Basics of Stage Combat: Unarmed – by Andrew Ashenden
Combat Mime – by J.D. Martinez
Essential Stage Fencing – by Edward Rozinsky
Fight Choreography – by F. Braun McAsh
Fight Chorography, The Art of Non-Verbal Dialogue – by John Kreng
Fight Directing for the Theatre – by J. Allen Suddeth
Fight Direction – by William Hobbs
Fight Write – by Carla Hoch
Fighting Words – edited by David Blixt

APPENDIX C ADDITIONAL RESOURCES

A History of Contemporary Stage Combat – by Brian LeTraunik
How to Stunt in Hollywood – by Amy Johnston, Melissa Spence, et al.
Lessons from The Maestro: Crafting a Successful Fight/Stunt Career in Theatre and Film – by David L. Boushey
Of Paces – by Payson Burt
The Screen Combat Handbook – by Kevin Inouye
So You Want To Be A Stuntman – by Robert Chapin
Stage Combat – Jenn Zuko Boughn
Stage Combat Arts – by Christopher Duval
The Stage Combat Handbook – Wolf Christian
Stage Combat Swordplay from Shakespeare to Present – by John Lennox
Stage Fighting – by Jonathan Howell
Staging Shakespeare's Violence – by Seth Duerr and Jared Kirby
Stunts: The How To Handbook – by Angela Meryl and Michael Andre Adams
Swashbuckling – by Richard Lane
The Swords of Shakespeare – by J.D. Martinez
The Theatrical Firearms Handbook – by Kevin Inouye
A Terrific Combat!!! – by Tony Wolf
The Textbook of Theatrical Combat – by Richard Pallaziol
Unarmed Stage Combat – by Philip d'Orleans

Books on Historical Combat

The Complete World Encyclopedia of Knives, Swords, Spears, and Daggers – Harvey Withers and Tobias Capwell
Fighting with the German Longsword – by Christian Henry Tobler
Secrets of German Medieval Swordsmanship – by Christian Henry Tobler
In Saint George's Name – by Christian Henry Tobler
The Art of Combat by Joachim Meyer – Translated by Jeffery L. Forgeng
Codex Wallerstein – by Gizegorz Zabinski, with Bartlomiej Walczak
The Beginner's Guide to the Long Sword – by Steaphen Fick
The Art of The Two Handed Sword – by Ken Mondschein
Medieval Swordsmanship – by John Clements
Sigmund Ringeek's Knightly Arts of Combat – by David Lindhom and Peter Svärd

The Martial Arts of Renaissance Europe – by Sydney Anglo
Sword Fighting – by Herbert Schmidt
The Book of the Sword – by Richard F. Burton
The Archaeology of Weapons – by Ewart Oakeshott
The Knightly Art of Battle – Ken Mondschein
Schools and Masters of Fencing – by Egerton Castle
Teaching and Interpreting Historical Swordsmanship – edited by Brian R. Price
The Secret History of the Sword – by J. Christoph Amberger
Hans Talhoffer Medieval Combat – Mark Rector
Lessons on the English Longsword – by Brandon P. Heslop and Benjamin G. Bradak
German Longsword Study Guide – by Keith Farrell & Alex Bourdas
Historical Fighting Fundamentals: German Longsword – by Kyle Griswold
Codex Amberger – by Dierk Hagedorn and Christophe Amburger
Jude Lew: Das Fechtbuch – by Dierk Hagedorn
Gladiatoria: New Haven – MS U860.F46 1450 – by Dierk Hagedorn and Bartłomiej Walczak
Dürer's Fightbook – by Dierk Hagedorn and Daniel Jaquet
The Art of Longsword Fighting – by Benjamin J Smith
Renaissance Combat, Jörg Wilhalm's Fightbook, 1522–1523 – by Dierk Hagedorn
Book of fencing skills – Paulus Hector Mair 1540–1550 – by Petr Turya

Books of Interest

Enter the Whole Army: A Pictorial Study of Shakespearean Staging, 1576–1616 – by C. Walter Hodges
The Body Keeps the Score – by Bessel van der Kolk
Movement Directors in Contemporary Theatre – by Ayse Tashkiran
Staging Sex – by Chelsea Pace
Staging Trauma – by Miriam Haughton
Supporting Staged Intimacy – by Alexis Black, Tina M. Newhauser

INDEX

Note: *Italic* page numbers refer to figures.

actions: advanced 114–126; beginning 67; closing 63, 121; concise 144–145; emotional 146–147; ending 68; killing 127–132; middle 67–68; physical 143–146
active blocks 85, 98–113; face, avoiding 98–99; on the high lines 99–102; historical *vs.* theatrical 98; on the low line 102–103; manipulation of 104–110
active footwork 143–144
active movement 143
active parry 111
advance 48, 49; left 53, 53; right 52, 53
aggressor 145
Alber (fool) 25
Archaeology of Weapons: Arms and Armor from Prehistory to the Age of Chivalry, The 10
attack: active 98–113; counterattack 25, 99, 101–103; false 118–120; flowing 107–108; lines of 69; normalising 78; point 78–80; pressure 104, 112; to the shoulders 100–101; zones of 22, 23
attacker 94, 97, 99, 100, 103, 105–109, 115–119, 121, 122, 124, 128–132, 134, 139
avoidance 61, 144

back edge 12
base stance 22–23, 24
bastard sword (hand-and-a-half sword) 9, 139
behind-the-back block 93, 94
belly swipe 117, *117*

Bibliotheque Nationale de France 5
bind 108–110
Binden *see* binding
binding 104
blade 11–12, *12*; awareness 60; thumbing-the-blade 21, *21*
blind parry 94
blocks 83–97; active (*see* active blocks); active blocks/attacks on the blade; edge *vs.* flat 84, 85; historical *vs.* theatrical 83; numbering *vs.* names 84; parries *vs.* 84; reinforced 94; static 85–97
body dynamics 59–60, 148–149
body engagement 60
broadsword 2, 9–10

casting 65
ceding parry *see* yielding parry
central ridge 11
change cut 119–120, *120*
chop cut 68
circling parry 100, *100*
circular cut 68
closed guards 42
closing actions 63, 121
closing distance 66, *66*
Codex Wallerstein (*Bauman Fechtbuch*) 6
Conan spin 137
contact killing cuts 130, *131*
corps-à-corps (body to body) 121
counterattack 25, 99, 101–103
croisé 108, 109, 134
cross-guard 11

cuts 63–82, 64; advanced 114–126; casting 65; change 119–120, 120; composition of 67–68; diagonal 75, 76; distance 65–66, 66; draw 63; historical sources of 63–65; lifting 101; Long-Sword 68–72; Method of Action 67; modern theatrical 65; to thrust 119; thrust to 119; vertical 76–78
cut-through drill 82
cutting drills: diagonal, with passing footwork 80–81; horizontal, with passing footwork 80–81; Meyer's Drill 81, 81
cut to the left hip 72; diagonal 75; horizontal 73–74, 73; static blocks 90, 91
cut to the left shoulder 68; diagonal 75, 76; head 76–77, 77; horizontal 70–71, 71; static blocks 88
cut to the right hip: diagonal 75; horizontal 72, 73; static blocks 90, 91
cut to the right shoulder 68; diagonal 75, 76; head 77–78, 77; horizontal 70, 70; static blocks 88

Danzig, Peter von 25
Dao 2
De Arte Gladiatoria Dimicandi (On the Art of Swordsmanship) 5–6
death grip 20
defense: zones of 22, 23
deflective parry 101
De Norske Vikingsverd ("The Norwegian Viking Swords") 10
Dente di zenghiaro (boar's tooth) 26, 38–39
Deritto [Dritto, Dritti, Mandritto] 64
diagonal cut 75, 76
disarms 132–136; dropping the sword 133–134; from the pris d'fer 134, 134; stomp 134, 134
disengage 104
displacements *see* thwarts
distance 16–17, 65–66, 145–146; closing 66, 66; In Distance 66, 66; killing cuts 128–129; Out of Distance 66, 66
downstage 151
draw cuts 63

draw-flip 138
dropping the sword: flat drop 133–134; tip-down drop 133

edge 11, 12
edge-to-edge parries 84
Einhorn (unicorn) 31, 33
elbow cut 67
emotional actions 146–147
engage 104
En Guard *see* On Guard
envelopment 108, 110
expulsions 110
eye contact 145

false attacks: stop short 118–119
false edge 12
Fechtbuch 6
feints *see* false attacks
fencing master 5
Fendenti [Fendente] 63
Fick, Steaphen 84
fight-line 23
fight-line *see* line of engagement
figure-8 spin 137
Fior di Battaglia (The Flower of Battle, Flos Duellatorum) 5
Fiore 64
fire swords 139
flair, adding 136–139
flat-front spin 138
Florius "de Arte Luctandi" 5
flowing attacks 107–108
flow of energy 148
Flyssa 2
foible 12, 85
footwork 45–59, 46; basic steps 46–48, 47–50; stepping up the game 48–54
forte 12, 85
froissements *see* pressure glide
front edge 12
fuller 12

general body posture 22, 23
Gladiatoria 6

INDEX

glissade 107–108, 108
Goliath Fechtbuch 7
grabbing 135, 135
grappling 121
grasp *see* holding
grip 11; death 20; hand-and-a-half 20, 21; reversing 139; single-hand 20, 21; two-handed 21, 21
Gründtliche Beschreibung, der freyen Ritterlichen unnd Adelichen kunst des Fechtens, in allerley gebreuchlichen Wehren, mit vil schönen und nützlichen Figuren gezieret und fürgestellet 7
guards 25; hanging 31–33, 31, 32, 74; high 26–30, 27–30; historical sources of 25–26; historical vs. stage 41; long vs. short 42; low 38–39, 39, 74; middle 33–37, 34–37; open vs. closed 42; positions 19; tail 40–41, 40, 74

half-swording 94, 120, 121; killing cuts 131; pummeling attacks 124
hand-and-a-half grip 20, 21
hanging guard: horizontal cut 74; left side 32; point attacks 79; posture of 31–32, 31; static blocks 88; variations of 33
hanging parries 87, 101
Hangort (hanging point) 31, 33
head swipe 117–118, 118
HEMA *see* Historical European Martial Arts
Hero's Parry 92, 93
high guard 26–30, 27–30; point attacks 79; posture of 27–28; variations of 28–30
High Left guard 26–28
high lines: active blocks on 99–102; horizontal cuts to 68–69, 71–72; reinforced blocks on 94–95, 95; static blocks on 86
High Right guard 26–28, 27
hilt 11, 11; bashes 63; smash (bash/strike) 121–122, 122
Historical European Martial Arts (HEMA) 1, 12, 13
history to stage and screen, taking 4–5
hit 140

holding 20–22
horizontal cuts: to the high line 68–69, 71–72; to the low line 72–74

implied violence 151–152
In Distance 66, 66
in-line *see* on-line
intention 41

J. Paul Getty Museum, Los Angeles, California 5
jumps 61

Kal, Paulus 25
Kasskara 2
Katana 1
Khepesh 2
kick off 133
killing actions 127–132
killing cuts: contact 130, 131; in distance 128–129; half-swording 131; noncontact 129–130, 130; out of distance 128, 129
killing thrusts: to torso 131–132, 132
knap 123
knock-away parry 101, 102, 102, 111
Krumphau (crooked strike) 125
Kunsthistorisches Museum, Vienna, Austria 6

leaning 61, 144
left dominant 24
leg swipes 116–117, 116
leveraging: sword down 135–136, 136; sword up 136, 137
Liberi, Fiore de'i 5
Liechtenauer, Johannes 5, 7
lifting cut 101
line of direction *see* fight-line
line of engagement 58
lines of attack 69
lines of sight 150–152
London and the Vikings 10
long guard 42
Long-Sword: cuts 68–72; offensive actions of 63

INDEX

low guard: horizontal cut 74; point attacks 80; posture of 38, 39; variations of 38–39
low lines: active blocks on 102–103; horizontal cuts to 72–74; static blocks on 90

Madmartigan flip 138–139
Mair, Paulus Hector 6–7
Marozzo, Achille 7, 26
Meisterhau 65, 125–126
method of action 67, 147–148
Meyer, Joachim 7; drill 81, 81
Mezani [Mezzane] 64
middle guard: left side 33–35, 34; point attacks 79; posture of 33, 34; static blocks 86; variations of 35–37, 35–37
Mittelhau (middle cuts) 64
modern training swords 12
Moulinet (Molinello) 76, 88
Myer, Joachim 25

Nebenhut (near ward) 25, 40
Nguyen, Qui: *She Kills Monsters* 94
noncontact killing cuts 129–130, 130
numbering vs. names 84

Oakeshott, Ewart 10
"Oakeshott Typology, The" 10
Oberhau (over cuts) 64
Ochs (ox) 25, 31; Left 88; Right 88
off-line/offline 41, 78
On Guard 33
on-line/online 41, 78
open guards 42
Opera Nova (*New Work*) 7
Out of Distance 66, 66
out of distance: killing cuts 128, 129

Pallaziol, Richard 84
parries 83–97; active 111; blind 94; blocks vs. 84; circling 100, 100; deflective 101; edge-to-edge 84; edge vs. flat 84, 85; hanging 87, 101; Hero's Parry 92, 93; historical vs. theatrical 83; knock-away 101, 102, 102, 111; numbering vs. names 84; passthrough 100, 111; reinforced static 94–95; striking 100, 101, 102, 111; yielding 108, 109
Parry 2 91
Parry 3 86, 94
Parry 4 86, 95
Parry 5 90, 95
Parry 5a 89, 95
Parry 7 91, 103
partnering 16
pass 46; back 46, 47; back left 50–51, 52; back right 50, 52; forward 46, 47; forward left 50, 51; forward right 50, 51
passthrough parry 100, 111
Pflug (plow) 25, 33
physical actions 143–146
physical reactions 148
physical reactions to pain 140–141
Pierpont Morgan Library, New York 5
Pisano, Philippo di Vadi 5–6
point 11; attacks 78–80, 79; thrusts 78–80
pommel 11; swing 124
pommel attack 63; to the body 123–124; to the face 122–123, 123; to the face, swinging 125; half-swording 124
Porta di ferro mezana (middle iron door) 26, 38, 168
Posta breve (short guard) 26, 33, 35–36, 35
Posta Coda Longa (long tail) 40
Posta di bicorno (two-horned guard) 26, 33, 37, 37
Posta di Coda lunga (long lying tail) 26
Posta di dente zenchiaro mezana (middle boar's tooth guard) 26, 38, 39
Posta di donna (woman's guard) 26, 29–30, 30
Posta di donna la sinestra (woman's guard on the left) 26, 30, 30
Posta di falcone (guard of the falcon) 26
Posta di finestro (window guard) 26, 31
Posta frontale ditta corona (crown guard) 26, 29, 29

INDEX

Posta longa (long guard) 33, 36–37, 36
press 105–106, 105, 112
pressure attacks 104, 112
pressure glide 106, 107, 112
pris d'fer 104, 108–110, 110, 112; disarm from the 134, 134
pronation 22

quick cut 68

reactions 147–149; physical 148
reinforced blocks 94; on the high line 94–95, 95
reinforced static parries 94–95, 95
retreat 48, 50; left 54, 55; right 54, 54
reversing grips 139
Ridoppio 64
right dominant 24
Ringeck, Sigmund 25
Riverso [Riversi, Roversi] 64
Romeo and Juliet 9, 15

safety 14–16, 114–115
Salzburg, Hans Medel von 25
Scheitelhau (parting strike) 126
Schielhau (squinter) 126
Shakespeare, William 9
short guard 42
shoulder cut 67
single-hand grip 20, 21
slashes 63
sloped parry *see* Hero's Parry
Sottani [Sotano] 64
speed 17–18, 145
Squalembrato 64
squats 61
stance 24–25; base 22–23, 24
Star Wars A New Hope 15
static blocks 85–97, 87; to the head 88–90; on high lines 86; on the low lines 90; to the shoulders 86–88, 87
stomp disarm 134, 134
stop short 118–119
striking parry 100, 101, 102, 111
supination 22

swipes 63, 69, 115–118, 115; base actions of 115–116; belly 117, 117; head 117–118, 118; leg 116–117, 116
swords: dropping 133–134; fire 139; flips 138–139; half-swording 120, 121, 124; spinning with 139; spins 137; taking 135–136; types of 9; *see also individual entries*

tail guard 40–41; horizontal cut 74; point attacks 80; posture of 40–41, 40; variations of 41
Takouba 2
Talhoffer, Hans 6, 25
tang 11
theatrical/film swords 12
theatrical violence, elements of: distance 16–17; partnering 16; safety 14–16; speed 17–18
thrust 63; to cut 119; cut to 119; point 78–80; to the torso, blocking 91, 92; to the torso, killing 131–132, 132
thumbing-the-blade 21, 21
thwart 54–58; backward left 58, 58; backward right 57, 57; forward left 57, 57; forward right 56, 56; left 55, 56; right 55, 56
Tobler, C. 5
transition 23
traverse 46; left 47–48, 49; right 46–47, 48
true edge 12, 68
Tutta porta di ferro (whole iron door) 26, 40, 41
two-handed grip 21, 21
two-sword sword fighting 139

Unterhau (under cuts) 64
upstage 151

Vadi 64
Valdi, Filippo 26
vertical attack: to the left shoulder 92; to the right shoulder 92
vertical cut: down to the head 76–78, 77; to the left shoulder 90; normalising

attacks 78; to the right shoulder 89; static blocking 89
Villa Pisani Dossi, Corbetta, Italy 5
violence: implied 151–152
violence *see* theatrical violence, elements of
vocal actions 149–150
vocal cue 94, 128
Volanti 64
Vom Tag [Dach/Tach/Tage] (from the roof) 25, 26

walk-through 17
wards *see* guards
warning 18
waterfall parry *see* Hero's Parry
weapon maintenance 18
Wilhalm, Jörg 6
winding 104
wrapping a finger over the guard 21, 21
wrist cut 67

yielding parry 108, 109

Zettel 5
Zornhau (strike of wrath) 125

For Product Safety Concerns and Information please contact our EU
representative GPSR@taylorandfrancis.com
Taylor & Francis Verlag GmbH, Kaufingerstraße 24, 80331 München, Germany

www.ingramcontent.com/pod-product-compliance
Lightning Source LLC
Chambersburg PA
CBHW052119300426

44116CB00010B/1719